Studies in Writing & Rhetoric

Other Books in the Studies in Writing & Rhetoric Series

Rhetoric and Reality: Writing Instruction in American Colleges, 1900–1985
James A. Berlin

Writing Instruction in Nineteenth-Century American Colleges
James A. Berlin

Something Old, Something New: College Writing Teachers and Classroom Change
Wendy Bishop

Variables of Composition: Process and Product in a Business Setting
Glenn J. Broadhead and Richard C. Freed

Audience Expectations and Teacher Demands
Robert Brooke and John Hendricks

Rehearsing New Roles: How College Students Develop As Writers
Lee Ann Carroll

Dialogue, Dialectic, and Conversation: A Social Perspective on the Function of Writing
Gregory Clark

Toward a Grammar of Passages
Richard M. Coe

A Communion of Friendship: Literacy, Spiritual Practice, and Women in Recovery
Beth Daniell

Embodied Literacies: Imageword and a Poetics of Teaching
Kristie S. Fleckenstein

Writing Groups: History, Theory, and Implications
Anne Ruggles Gere

Computers & Composing: How the New Technologies Are Changing Writing
Jeanne W. Halpern and Sarah Liggett

Teaching Writing as a Second Language
Alice S. Horning

Women Writing the Academy: Audience, Authority, and Transformation
Gesa E. Kirsch

Invention as a Social Act
Karen Burke LeFevre

A New Perspective on Cohesion in Expository Paragraphs
Robin Bell Markels

Gender Influences: Reading Student Texts
Donnalee Rubin

The Young Composers: Composition's Beginnings in Nineteenth-Century Schools
Lucille M. Schultz

Technology and Literacy in the Twenty-First Century: The Importance of Paying Attention
Cynthia L. Selfe

Language Diversity in the Classroom: From Intention to Practice
Edited by Geneva Smitherman and Victor Villanueva

Across Property Lines: Textual Ownership in Writing Groups
Candace Spigelman

Mutuality in the Rhetoric and Composition Classroom
David L. Wallace and Helen Rothschild Ewald

Evaluating College Writing Programs
Stephen P. Witte and Lester Faigley

Response to Reform

Response to Reform

Composition and the
Professionalization
of Teaching

Margaret J. Marshall

SOUTHERN ILLINOIS UNIVERSITY PRESS
Carbondale

Copyright © 2004 by the Conference on College Composition and
Communication of the National Council of the Teachers of English
All rights reserved
Printed in the United States of America
07 06 05 04   4 3 2 1

Publication partially funded by a subvention grant from The Conference on College Composition and Communication of the National Council of the Teachers of English.

Library of Congress Cataloging-in-Publication Data

Marshall, Margaret J.
  Response to reform : composition and the professionalization of teaching / Margaret J. Marshall.
      p. cm. — (Studies in writing & rhetoric)
  Includes bibliographical references (p.) and index.
  1. English language—Rhetoric—Study and teaching—United States. 2. Report writing—Study and teaching (Higher)—United States. 3. Sex discrimination in higher education—United States. 4. Sexism in higher education—United States. 5. Feminism and education—United States. 6. Educational change—United States. 7. English teachers—United States. I. Title. II. Series.
  PE1405.U6M37 2003
  808'.042'071173—dc21   2003006164
  ISBN 0-8093-2545-4 (alk. paper)

Printed on recycled paper.

The paper used in this publication meets the minimum requirements of American National Standard for Information Sciences—Permanence of Paper for Printed Library Materials, ANSI Z39.48-1992.

for my many teachers,
but especially for the two who are also my children,
Caleb and Kileen

Contents

Acknowledgments — xi

1. Survival from a Time Now Dead — 1
2. Fit to Keep School — 18
3. Reshaping Professional Training — 63
4. A Mere Factory Hand — 93
5. Standing to Speak — 143

Works Cited — 183

Index — 191

Acknowledgments

This project has been evolving for a number of years. Along the way, I have had much support, good advice, and more than a few friendly readers. Early archival research at the Chicago Historical Society was funded in part by a travel grant from the University of Pittsburgh. Generous grants from Provost Luis Glaser at the University of Miami allowed me to complete the research and finish the manuscript during the summers of 2001 and 2002. Throughout the process, Robert Brooke has encouraged me to take this project in new directions, pushed me to write more when I thought there was nothing left to be said, and patiently waited for the manuscript as I moved to a new position and took on new responsibilities. Robert's ability to find generous and helpful reviewers is a testament to his deep understanding of what writers need and how members of our profession can draw on their own interests to offer critical responses. I would especially like to thank John Brereton and Yuet-Sim Chiang for their encouragement to rethink specific features of the text; they urged me to do more when I desperately wanted to be finished, but they were right that the book needed those last efforts.

Of course, friends, colleagues, and family members also provided support throughout this project. Terry and Ginny Purvis-Smith graciously opened their home to me when I went to Chapel Hill to do archival research at the University of North Carolina. Some of my first efforts to track the history of teacher education were helped by women colleagues in a writing group at the University of Pittsburgh, particularly Mariolina Salvatori, Jean Ferguson Carr, Nancy Glazener, and Paula Kane. Shari Benstock listened to ideas in formation, included me in the SUCCEED project, and asked me about my work with patience and goodwill. Perri Lee Roberts read and responded to an early draft of what became parts of the first two chapters. Her interest helped me see that this project might speak to readers even outside English studies. Anne Ruggles Gere provided me with encouragement and suggestive leads to follow. Joy Ritchie, Tassie Gwilliam, and Cheryl Glenn inspired me with their own thoughtful scholarship in related areas and generously allowed me to talk through interpretations still in formation. John Paul Russo cheerfully inquired after the project on a regular basis and lent a good ear to title possibilities. Deborah Minter has read much of this work in bits and pieces as it developed, helped me through the moments of discouragement, and celebrated the high points like the good friend she is.

Many of the non-tenure-track faculty that I have had the pleasure of working with at the University of Pittsburgh and the University of Miami have helped me think through the complications of administrative work and program development in ways that also helped me with this project. I would especially like to thank Gina Maranto, April Mann, Carol Bott, John Wafer, Andrew Strycharski, James Britton, and Anita Daniels. Likewise, the graduate students taking the "Teaching Seminars" at the University of Pittsburgh and then at the University of Miami taught me more than they can imagine about the professionalization of teaching and the preparation of graduate students for classroom work. Clara Maroney, the senior staff associate for the composition program at the University of Miami, has helped in numerous ways with this project, especially by keeping other parts of my professional life from spinning out of control. My husband, Randall, has been a constant supporter, cooking meals so I could write, entertaining the children so I could stay in the archives, and reading the entire manuscript with an eye for detail that only a lawyer could maintain. Finally, my stepmother, Wanda Proctor, my father, Arnold Gray Proctor, my mother-in-law, Selma Margaret Marshall, and my children, Caleb and Kileen, asked about my progress, encouraged me to keep working, and pitched in to help with household chores at key moments in this long process. To all these people, I owe a debt of gratitude. All mistakes are, of course, my own.

Response to Reform

1 / Survival from a Time Now Dead

During the 1884 National Education Association meeting in Madison, Wisconsin, a meeting that was the largest gathering of American educators to that date, a "women's evening" was held with four speakers delivering addresses at one of two simultaneous meetings. One of those speakers, May Wright Sewall, began her speech with an acknowledgment of the special opportunity for women to speak before the convention. Previous conventions had included a single woman as a keynote speaker at the general sessions and some department meetings (especially the Normal Schools Department and the Elementary Schools Department) had regular presentations by women, but the special women's evening was one of the innovations that President Thomas W. Bicknell used to increase attendance at the convention. Sewall, a high school teacher who had begun the Girls' Classical School of Indianapolis with her husband two years before, called the occasion "a survival from a time now dead, when every church held its distinct corner for distinct and inferior classes" (Sewall 153). Though Sewall went on to say that she was certain the men occupying the platform with her and welcoming the women to speak did not consider the women to be "inferior" or "curiosities," it is difficult not to hear in those words a tongue-in-cheek critique of the power structures that relegated these women to a special, but clearly marginalized, position within the convention and the organization that hosted it.

Such self-consciousness about the limited participation of women teachers in the hierarchy of the major professional organization of the time was unusual, but not unknown. As early as the 1875 convention, Delia A. Lathrop, the principal of the Training School in Cincinnati, Ohio, had noted in her speech before the Normal Schools Department: "it should never be forgotten, that in discussing the professional education of teachers, we are indirectly considering the question of the professional education of women," and that "any plan for the professional education of teachers in this country that does not take into account the peculiar circumstances of women in these relations will fail of the highest success" (Lathrop 140, 141).

The words used at events more than a hundred years ago may seem to have little to do with present-day interests, problems, or situations, but consider for a moment the current discussions about the use of adjunct faculty as teachers of required first-year composition courses. These discussions regularly point out the predominance of women in these underpaid, marginalized teaching positions. Likewise, while most members of the academic world take great pains to insist on the equality of women, there is no escaping the evidence that though more women receive advanced degrees, fewer of them are granted tenure or promotion. In fact, because composition is a field that centers itself around undergraduate teaching, the prejudices against both teaching and women may compound the effects of long-standing academic hierarchies and the unexamined assumptions that support these practices. Thus, like Sewall, I want to suggest that some of what we do, say, and think has been inherited from a time now dead, even if we do not intend to support the prejudices of a prior era. Furthermore, I contend that without some level of self-consciousness about this inheritance, we will continue to repeat, unwittingly, the patterns of discourse that have generated the very conditions we wish to alter or refute.

This is a book, then, about language, history, and practice. It is about the connections, or distinctions, that we inherit from a previous time in the language and cultural conceptions that continue to shape our world and our understandings. More specifically, it is about how the current debates within higher education in the United States that are connected with the literacy work of composition studies might profit by a closer examination of the discourses of the past, and a consideration of our rhetorical choices. Such an examination allows us to reconceptualize what it means to prepare for and enter the profession, especially the relationship between scholarship and teaching. Such an examination also repositions those of us who have *chosen* to teach the literacy of written discourse as something other than powerless victims.

This book makes several claims, among them

- that composition instruction at the university is the newest level of literacy expectation and thus the newest expectation of common schooling in American culture;
- that with the expectation for a new level of literacy, and a concomitant level of common schooling, higher education has received increased attention and criticism in the public discourse;
- that this scrutiny and criticism follows a pattern of quickly turning from worrying about education in general to a criticism of teachers and teaching;
- that the response to public criticism is most often a call for teachers to be "professionalized" through specialized programs of training and certification;
- that these programs—partly because of class and gender prejudices, partly because of the logistical difficulties of providing qualified teachers for the increased numbers of students, and partly because of the contradictions between professional values and the bureaucratic structure of educational institutions—do not manage to educate teachers in ways that allow them to assume the independent decision making essential to claiming the status of professionals, thus setting the stage for the next call to reform by professionalizing teachers anew;
- that attempts to reeducate literacy teachers are regularly accompanied by efforts to draw attention to material conditions that exploit teachers and marginalize their work; the argument that improving material conditions will lead to improved teaching, however, has to date relied on a rhetoric of labor that further distances teachers from the power of professionalism and reinforces the controls of management;

- that these historical patterns constitute a set of rhetorical tropes that are largely unexamined, but remain with us, tainting subsequent efforts to alter the situation and recreating the contradictions that prevent meaningful reform;
- that attention to the history, the language, the contradictions we inherit from a time now dead, can allow us to break the cycle and reconceptualize teaching, professionalization, and responses to public criticism of education differently and perhaps more successfully.

While the chapters that follow provide elaboration and exemplars of these central historical patterns, there are two key terms that must be explicated here: *literacy* and *professionalism*. Neither of these terms is simple, and both have their own patterns of development and scholarly controversy that figure as the background to this study of the professionalization of teaching as a response to public criticism of education. It is to that explication that I now turn.

Background: Literacy and Schooling

Here's my first assertion: those of us who teach composition to undergraduates are engaged in the newest level of common school literacy. What follows is a summary of the evidence that leads to this conclusion.

Although *literacy* is a term commonly used to mean the decoding skills necessary to read a written text, literacy researchers like Lawrence Stedman and Carl Kaestle point out that "[l]iteracy is not a single skill, but a set of skills that people have to varying degrees" (10). Indeed, what it means to be "literate" and how researchers measure the literacy abilities of past or present populations are matters of debate within literacy scholarship. As Kaestle explains in his 1985 review of literacy research, historians must extrapolate literacy abilities from such evidence as wills or marriage registers signed with names or marked with an *X*, but whether people who could sign their own names were able to write other documents or read texts is often a matter of considerable speculation. Schooling practices differ by location, class, and gender, so that if students learned to read first, poorer students who left school before writing was introduced might have signed documents with an *X* even though they knew how to read. When reading and writing were learned simultaneously and given equal priority, however, the correlation between signature records and adult reading abilities is probably greater. But, because some students who learn to read have little opportunity to do so, reading (and perhaps writing) ability can be lost over time. Likewise, relying on self-reporting of literacy ability is riddled with the social stigmas attached to illiteracy, stigmas that apparently increase as the general level of literacy increases (Clifford 473).

Geraldine Clifford's 1984 review of the evolution of literacy and its connections to schooling outlines changes in literacy along three dimensions (482). First, Clifford shows that to be literate in Western civilization has meant, at different periods, the ability to (1) sign your own name; (2) read familiar text; (3) read unfamiliar text in order to gain information; and, (4) most recently, perform "higher-order thinking skills" such as interpretation and analysis. Second, Clifford demonstrates that each time the general population achieves the expected level of literacy, the definition of literacy shifts to a higher level. Thus, the number of people considered literate grows until the majority of the population achieves that level of literacy, and then the expected level of literacy rises and the process begins again. Finally, Clifford suggests that "the social and individual purposes that literacy is intended to serve" have expanded to include economic, civic and social interactions not previously required (482–90). Reading biblical texts in unison and knowing the principles of a denomination's beliefs was meant to support the authority of the religious hierarchy; reading to make one's own interpretations, question an authority, and support judgments of one's own in a written text—as today's critical literacy demands—positions individuals very differently.

Determining the causes or the results of literacy development in either individuals or nations is thus a complicated undertaking.

When literacy, whatever its definition, is widespread enough to be perceived as a valuable tool, it becomes culturally significant, and the population has developed what Clifford calls a "literacy consciousness" (472). Such a literacy consciousness shapes a culture's institutional structures, political and social interactions, and values. For example, in the United States, the demand for literacy and its perceived value has generated a consistent pressure to expand schooling opportunities. By the 1780s, 75–90 percent of white men could sign their names to official documents (Kaestle 27, 30). Female literacy rates at this date were slightly less, but have been estimated at 60–90 percent, depending on the level of commerce in the region and the proximity of the family to schooling (Kaestle 29–30). Such widespread basic literacy marks the literacy consciousness Clifford identifies, and, true to form, the arguments for public common schooling began to intensify in the years surrounding the start of the nineteenth century.

Increased availability of schooling supports the American ideology of individual meritocracy, but this same expanded availability of schooling generates anxiety among the middle class. John Trimbur has argued that the recurring "literacy crisis" and the concurrent public criticism of schools is the result of an ideology that uses reading and writing abilities as a means of sorting the population into "masters" and "servants" (280). When larger portions of the population gain access to schooling, and thus access to literacy, the middle class's "fears of falling" create a public pressure that makes additional schooling or higher levels of literacy an entrance requirement for management and professional employment even if those levels are not essential for the specific occupation. Increasing levels of literacy may not, Trimbur argues, be signs of simple evolution or progress, but rather an ongoing attempt by the middle class to maintain the hierarchies and privileges of economic security and professional status.

In 1910, when 50 percent of American students had completed the eighth grade, a literacy level of fifth grade is probably a more accurate indicator of the ability of most who left school (Clifford 491). Because many schools at that time used rote memorization and oral recitation for literacy instruction, students were not generally expected to read for independent comprehension or to apply information. During World War I, standardized tests administered to 1.7 million GIs revealed that 30 percent could not read well enough to understand the test (Resnick and Resnick 381). Of course, reading information independently and understanding it well enough to answer questions about content or apply the information to a problem represents a much higher level of literacy than signing a name or recognizing familiar printed words well enough to say them aloud. But this new level of literacy became the expected norm after World War I, and, not coincidentally, length of schooling steadily increased. High school attendance among people aged 14–17 rose from 6.7 percent in 1890 to 33 percent in 1920, from 51 percent in 1930 to 92.3 percent in 1981 (Clifford 491; Kliebard 17).

In the 1980s, a similar "crisis" in literacy appeared in the public and professional press as comparisons with other countries apparently revealed that American high school students lagged behind their contemporaries in Japan and Europe. Of course, the literacy then considered acceptable was again more advanced than what had been considered acceptable previously. Students were measured not only on reading comprehension and application of information to new contexts but also for the ability to write coherent and argumentative prose, synthesize data from different sources, and make critical judgments. Despite attempts to call attention to the problems of standardized testing and the possibility that no real crisis existed but merely an expansion of the population of students taking the exam (Ohmann; Shor; Sledd), pressure to improve schools continued through the 1980s and 1990s.

Meanwhile, within higher education, attention to writing ability increased steadily throughout the twentieth century. Educational historians have repeatedly characterized the colleges before the emergence of the university as employing an oral culture (Cremin; Hofstadter and Smith; Veysey). Students entering in a given year all took the same courses at the same time. Oral recitation was the common form of instruction and evaluation, and even lectures were reserved for senior seminars. Students in nineteenth-century colleges did not have open access to university libraries, and while Brereton (*Origins* 4) concludes that there were opportunities for writing, none of the evidence suggests that students in the nineteenth century wrote the kinds of independent research and critical arguments that are common in first-year composition programs today. In fact, one reason for the emergence of secret societies, student clubs, fraternities, and debate and literary groups on college campuses in the nineteenth century was students' desires for access to books and opportunities for more independent speaking and writing. Even the newest scholarship in the history of higher education, like that represented by the collection of essays edited by Roger Geiger, confirms this structure of orality and the importance of student-generated alternatives.

When Harvard University instituted a required first-year rhetoric and composition course in 1872, several features of modern university literacy instruction coalesced. First, it was President Charles W. Eliot's intention to create a structure of higher education that would support research and advance knowledge. Creating departments organized around disciplinary knowledge and allowing students to take a variety of elective courses rather than a regimented curriculum were two of his innovations. Second, Eliot was interested in altering the curriculum of high schools and preparatory schools in a way that would allow colleges to concentrate on more advanced study. Third, to compete with other disciplines within this new structure of higher education, English needed to have a specific body of knowledge and a set of research methods that could designate the expertise of professors rather than a set of literacy skills that would be imparted to students. Thus, Eliot appointed a lawyer turned newspaper reporter, Adams Sherman Hill, to relieve the German-trained Ph.D. Francis James Child from the work of reading student themes. This appointment set the stage for what has become the ongoing devaluing of both composition and the teaching of undergraduates, a historical construction of literature as "high" and composition as "low," which is well outlined in Susan Miller's 1991 *Textual Carnivals*.

In keeping with the pattern visible in the expansion of lower levels of public schooling, the number of students attending colleges increased rapidly from 1890 to 1900. Geiger provides statistical evidence to show that the total number of students attending colleges and universities rose from 97,945 in 1890 (1.499 percent of the population aged 15–19) to 167,998 in 1900 (2.22 percent of the college-aged population) (269). Likewise, the kinds of students attending college expanded throughout the twentieth century, first to include more male students from successful working-class families, then to include more women. As has been well established, the open-admission policies of the 1970s expanded college enrollment even further to include more racial, ethnic, and class diversity than had been typical to that point. Figures for 1997 show 92.8 percent of the 14–17-year-olds were enrolled in grades 9–12 and 47 percent of the students who had graduated high school four years before finished an undergraduate degree that year (U.S. Census Bureau). In 1998, then President Bill Clinton declared in his state of the union address that with the efforts to offer grants to students and tax breaks for the middle class, college could be "as universal in the 21st century as high school is today."

Obviously, then, the kinds of literacy taught and practiced even among the most elite have changed over time. Likewise, the availability of higher education to larger segments of the population can be seen as a part of the pattern of American ideology that promises rewards based on individual merit, uses literacy abilities to sort those individuals, and fosters increasing levels of education to ensure the status of the middle class. The expanded opportunities for schooling and increasing levels of literacy have now met in the location of first-year college composition and its expectations for critical academic arguments.

Background: Professionalization and Teaching

When access to education expands, there is, of course, a need for more teachers. And, when expectations for literacy instruction increase, what teachers must know also increases. At each stage of expanded schooling and increasing levels of literacy, public and professional attention has quickly moved from generalized complaints about literacy and schooling to criticism of teachers and their teaching. This criticism of teachers and teaching regularly produces a call to professionalize teachers through a program of reeducation, state-controlled certification or licenses, and supervision and evaluation of classroom practices. Here, then, is my second claim: the efforts to professionalize teachers have actually denied teachers professional status because they have not included the kinds of education that would allow teachers to make independent, informed judgments, an essential function of a professional.

Studies of professionalization and the marks of professional status have proliferated during this century. The first historical studies of the phenomenon of professionalization began in the 1930s with Carr-Saunders and Wilson's book *The Professions*. In the 1970s, sociologists and historians brought Marxist analysis to the consideration of professional status and profession making. Scholars have now traced profession making back to its medieval origins, examined the role of women in various fields, and argued about the influence of professions, professional organizations, and professional expertise (see, e.g., Freidson; Haber; Haskel; Larson; Vollmer and Mills). Most scholars agree that there are several key features that distinguish professions from other occupations, including:

- direct control over entry into the profession (usually through specialized education also controlled by members of the profession in a postgraduate degree program);
- specialized language and procedures;
- journals and organizations;
- status and salary levels at a higher level than nonprofessionals in a similar occupation (attorneys versus paralegals, for example);
- freedom to exercise independent judgments in carrying out the specialized work of the profession in keeping with the accepted routines, practices, and ethics of the profession; and,

- questions about the performance (or ethics) of individual practitioners being handled by colleagues representing the profession.

Some scholars have noted that the term *profession* and its various cognates are applied to a wide variety of occupations to denote the effort to advertise expertise (professional dry cleaners, for example), full-time rather than amateur commitment to a particular activity (as in professional sports), or the desire to claim the status and prestige of more traditional professions (e.g., professional hairdressers). This casual use of *profession* led Howard Becker to suggest in 1962 that

> [w]e can, instead [of trying to devise an accurate definition], take a radically sociological view, regarding professions simply as those occupations which have been fortunate enough in the politics of today's work world to gain and maintain possession of that honorific title. On this view, there is no such thing as the "true" profession and no set characteristics necessarily associated with the title. There are only those work groups which are commonly regarded as professions and those which are not.
>
> Such a definition takes as central the fact that "profession" is an honorific title, a term of approbation. It recognizes that "profession" is a collective symbol and one that is highly valued. It insists that "profession" is not a neutral and scientific concept but, rather, what Turner has called a *folk concept*, a part of the apparatus of the society we study, to be studied by noting how it is used and what role it plays in the operations of that society. (32–33, emphasis in original)

Burton Bledstein's history of American higher education takes a similarly skeptical view of what he calls the "culture of professionalism," wherein middle class Victorian values were embodied by university presidents at the end of the nineteenth century, and those presidents, in turn, created an institutional structure that reinforced the authority, expertise, and prestige desired by the growing numbers of educated, middle-class men. Originally, the power of the traditional professions of law, medicine, and theology was justified by the unquestioned morality of the men who held those positions because they had the class standing to do so (see Legatt). But in American ideology, men were supposed to be equal; individual merit rather than inherited class standing was to be the measure of success and ability. Thus, Americans had to develop a system in which those without the traditional upper-class standing could acquire the values associated with professionals. The university system established by men like Charles Eliot of Harvard relied on the meritocracy necessary to the democratic ideology of Americans, allowed individuals to "get ahead" both financially and socially in a capitalistic economy, and still maintained the ideological values of service, sacrifice, expertise, and character associated with professions and the upper-class men who were, traditionally, professionals. In Eliot's plan for higher education, Susan Miller argues, the study of vernacular language and literature represented in the department of English was central to inculcating these upper-class values, and the first-year composition course became a means of sorting and retraining the not-yet-authorized beginning student.

Roger Kimball's study of the professional ideal contributes some interesting complications to the view of professionals as self-serving, status-seeking, middle-class men. Kimball argues that the meaning of *profession* changed over time, taking on the values and associations of the vocation considered the preeminent occupation of the time. So, for example, in the colonial era when clergy were thought to be the most outstanding citizens, professionals were those men ordained to speak publicly (from the pulpit) and to serve the community selflessly. Junior clergy, waiting for an assignment to their own church, or those clergy who could not speak effectively from the pulpit, served as schoolteachers. Thus, even before the common school movement increased the demand for teachers that necessitated women entering the classroom, those who taught were seen as either apprentices waiting for something better or inferiors who could do little else. Paul Mattingly also establishes the links between the evangelical roots of teaching and the professionalization of education, with a focus on school*men;* female teachers receive only passing mention because they were not considered "legitimate" members of the profession even when they outnumbered men in the classroom and as students at normal schools.

When law became the most highly regarded occupation after the Revolutionary War, Kimball argues, "service" as a professional value was transformed into that which was a "benefit to a client" (148) and the common use of the term *professed* declined, with *professional* taking its place as the term to refer to occupations. Such a shift in the language, Kimball argues, reflects the shift away from the vows necessary for joining the clergy and the demands on clergy to *profess* their faith publicly. This shift coincides with the common school movement, the beginnings of the feminization of classroom teaching, and the first references to school teaching being called a profession (Kimball 189), so it seems no small coincidence that *profession* no longer required public speaking, an activity that Barbara Harris shows even the most enlightened advocates of female education generally thought improper for women.

For Kimball, the shift in interests and prestige from polity to science, and the systematic organization of knowledge represented by growth in university study in the second half of the nineteenth century, coincides with the rise of education as the preeminent calling (200). The university also played an important role in the professionalization of other occupations because specialized study and obtaining a degree as a requirement for entry into a profession became accepted practice. Like Bledstein, however, Kimball collapses university professors and the scientific or systematic organization of knowledge they represent with the profession called *education,* dropping in the process the distinctions between schools and colleges and ignoring the large number of women who functioned as teachers but rarely as professors.

In fact, even the women who served as principals or professors in the normal schools in the nineteenth century do not seem to have expected public recognition of their work in these roles or to have referred to themselves as professionals. The case of Electa Lincoln Walton is particularly revealing in this regard, though she worked earlier in the nineteenth century. Walton served as principal of the public Normal School at West Newton, Massachusetts, when the then principal, Cyrus Peirce, fell ill in 1849. Although Peirce recommended Walton as his successor and everyone agreed she led the school well during the two terms she served as its principal, she willingly stepped aside for a man to assume the position and continued to work at the school as his assistant until she married a year later. She was not so amenable, however, to having her name omitted from the textbooks she and her husband authored together a few years later. Beverly Weiss reports that the publisher's insistence that her name be omitted so radicalized Walton that she became an outstanding spokesperson for women's rights even though subsequent editions of the texts included her name as coauthor. How women during this time conceptualized their right to professional status or to public recognition for their work or their words certainly deserves further study. It is unlikely, of course, that such perceptions were consistent across the large numbers, regions, and classes of women who taught, or even across the years of a single woman's life. As I demonstrate in subsequent chapters, the tensions inherent in women doing work that was in many ways *professional* (and therefore inappropriate for women) created contradictions that had no easy resolutions, but that often led to teaching being seen as nonprofessional, merely "women's work."

When Eliot created the modern American university a quarter of a century later, teaching was further relegated to secondary status behind research, a hierarchy clearly visible in the split between literary study and the teaching of first-year composition. The familiar story of Harvard's Boylston Chair of Rhetoric Francis Child being released from responsibility for teaching, or correcting, freshman writing in order to concentrate on literary research is generally taken as evidence of this hierarchy within English studies, a hierarchy that treats composition and teaching as lesser. By appointing

Adams Sherman Hill to supervise the first-year course, employing women in the work of disciplining the language use of beginning students and keeping these women in a lesser and separate status from literature professors, Susan Miller argues, Harvard established a set of common practices that feminized composition, and, I would add, kept it from claiming professional status from the moment of its creation in American higher education (Miller "Feminization").

Kimball's examination of the shifts in language and associations of profession does not counter the negative associations and antiprofessionalism that coexist with the status and privilege of professionals. In public discourse, this antiprofessionalism takes the form of jokes about the self-serving, money-hungry lawyers or suspicions about the value of the professional's book learning. In academic circles, *professionalization* often suggests the institutional structures that produce uniformity, a set of socially prescribed discourse practices that keeps individuals from thinking independently. Moreover, academics have a deep suspicion of professions and the prestige associated with professional status founded in part by observations like those of Barbara and John Ehrenreich, who note that professions do not emerge unless there is a problem that professionals can then solve. As Stanley Fish has demonstrated, however, even antiprofessionalism is built out of the values of individual merit central to professional ideology. In other words, criticizing the organizations and social and institutional structures that make up professional ideology is but another example of insisting on the importance of individual merit, and individual merit is the central feature of professional ideology. Thus for Fish, the criticism of professionalism is simply another affirmation of professional ideology.

Whether we consider professionalism positive or negative, the question of how people learn to be professionals has been largely ignored. Sociologists are satisfied to note that becoming a professional requires education or specific training.

Historians might trace the rise of particular kinds of institutions for that education, but they give little attention to the specifics of the curriculum or the pedagogy. If professionals must be able to make independent judgments and rise through individual merit, how do they learn to make these decisions and how are such decisions evaluated? And, if a discipline like composition has been denied professional status since its creation in American higher education because of its subservient relationship to literary study, how can those who choose this career path avoid the powerlessness of this pre-scripting?

Long-standing patterns of criticism and the efforts to reform teachers have now moved to the university level, our newest level of common schooling. These patterns are particularly visible in composition studies because it is there that the literacy expectations of common schooling intersect with traditions that value scholarship over teaching and that deny professional status to "women's work." In the chapters that follow, I examine the rhetorical constructions that linked together these threads (limited intellectual preparation, assumptions about gender that translated to the work of classroom teaching, the feminization of teaching, and the subservient role of undergraduate writing instruction at the university level). By turning to current efforts to reform higher education, I demonstrate that historic tensions have now come together with other features of modern work life that are commonly considered antithetical to professionalism (concern with material conditions, political advocacy, and unity through unionization), to make reconceptualizing the work of university faculty more difficult than these reforms acknowledge.

Obviously, elementary and secondary school teaching are not completely congruent with the teaching and scholarly activities of university professors, but the rhetoric that constructs the "work" of teaching, like the arguments to reposition that work, repeat many of the features of the prior discourses about classroom teachers and teaching at lower levels. Likewise, the history that constructed composition as beneath literary study cannot be ignored, but neither is it sensible to ignore the changes in epistemology, cultural values, and literacy practices that constitute more current disciplinary relationships. It is my contention that by attending to the echoes of prior discourses and being conscious of the ways language and argument construct (and limit) our conceptions, we will find ourselves in a better position to engage the discourses of the current debates and imagine possibilities that have not yet been suggested. With such rhetorical knowledge, that is, the power of choice may make all the difference in response to reform.

2 / Fit to Keep School

When the 1998 Boyer Commission on Educating Undergraduates in the Research University included in its suggestions a call for greater attention to the preparation graduate students receive to become university teachers, it repeated a pattern that has existed in public discussions of education since at least 1789. That pattern begins, as I explained in the first chapter, with concern about the quality of education that links literacy levels in particular, and education in general, to the economic prosperity of the nation and the political stability of democracy, as well as to the success of individuals. The criticism is associated with the middle class's anxiety about its own continuing success, expanding access to education, and increasing literacy expectations. While the criticism routinely prompts various solutions in the form of structural changes and curriculum revisions, it is the attention to teaching, teachers, and the preparation teachers receive before beginning their work in classrooms that is of most interest in this project. Here is my third claim: although the attempts to improve education by improving teachers has employed the rhetoric of professionalization, these efforts have not provided the kind of education that enables teachers to make independent judgments that qualify them as professionals.

The Boyer report, which moves this call for professionalizing teaching to the newest level of common education, the university, repeats a pattern of rhetorical constructions that suggests its efforts, too, will fail to alter the cultural structures that devalue teaching and teachers. Before I can examine the Boyer report, however, it is necessary to examine the features of this historical discourse about professionalizing teachers that establishes the pattern of language, argument, and conceptualization that remains in current discussions.

This chapter traces a history in which the literacy consciousness that precipitates an expansion of schooling, and therefore an increased demand for teachers, also generates public discussions about teaching and teachers that involve several simultaneous rhetorical moves, including

- a shift in the complaints about education to focus more specifically on the faults of teachers;
- a call for reforming (meaning improving) schools through a better system of preparing teachers for their classroom duties; and
- articulations of preparatory programs that alter the underlying definition of teaching from primarily knowledge or skill transfer to interactions with learners that require special expertise about child development, learning, and theories of teaching, expertise that allows writers to claim that teaching will be a profession.

These rhetorical constructions of teaching are, however, riddled with contradictions indicative of culturally valued but contested terms, and the actual attempts to put preparatory programs into place are hampered by economic, class, and logistical realities. The key features of these contradictions can be enumerated.

1. Because communities cannot provide the large numbers of teachers necessary for an expanded school system unless they keep the pay for these teachers low, teaching is opened to lower-class, less literate, and less respected individuals—including women—individuals not already associated with the higher status of professionals.

2. Because these new kinds of teachers have less prior education and are less likely to already have the values associated with professionals, preparatory programs must provide basic literacy, rather than specialized knowledge, and instill middle-class values, further undercutting the claim that teaching has professional status.

3. Gendering teaching as "women's work" further hampers efforts to provide a professional education because of the cultural

assumptions about women's capacities, their unsuitability for public roles, and their "natural" proclivity to nurture and serve others. 4. Thus, education becomes a profession through the development of an elaborate hierarchy whereby organizations, journals, supervision, research, and training programs are controlled by men, but teaching is firmly tied to the marginal, nonintellectual, and powerless status associated with the majority of classroom teachers who come to do this "women's work."

To trace these arguments and developments, I use examples from a wide range of public documents, including popular magazines, government reports and legislative actions, curriculum of early teaching institutes, diaries of early teachers of teachers, examinations and licensing standards for teachers, and records of early professional education organizations. The eclecticism of this evidence is not meant to suggest irrefutable proof of these claims, but rather to serve as exemplars of the inherited discourse that constitutes our own conceptions of teaching and the terrain against which we make our own arguments for reform and improvement. Finally, the most persistent features of this cultural conception are that teaching is not intellectual work, does not require special expertise separate from subject matter knowledge, and thus has no ground on which to claim professional status.

Increasing Teachers

As the new nation settled into the business of unification after the Constitution was ratified, public concern about schools and the ability of teachers to instill a set of common values and a national identity began to emerge. If the schools were to do this important cultural work, there would have to be more of them, and students would have to be taught more consistently. The June 1789 edition of the *Massachusetts Magazine,* a popular general magazine of the period, contains what Henry Barnard claims was the first public argument in America for a special school to prepare teachers (21). Addressed to the editor as a letter entitled "Importance of Education," the anonymous writer argues for providing all children in America a "common English education" with "a thorough knowledge of arithmetic and our own language, together with elegancy of reading and a fair legible hand" (382 n). After providing this explanation of "common education," the writer goes on in a footnote to say:

> Since education has been a question of much debate in this as well as in many of the other states, and what method is best to be adopted in order to lessen every unnecessary expense, yet to establish our schools on a more respectable footing than they have ever yet been; and to diffuse light and knowledge more universally among the people, I beg leave to suggest the following plan: As each town of a hundred and forty families, in this commonwealth, is obliged by an act of the General Court, to support a publick [sic] grammar school, in which it is very seldom you will find more than three or four boys, studying the learned languages; and as these scholars are the only persons who realize the extraordinary expense the town is at, in obtaining a master, qualified for the office; and, as, perhaps nine tenths of the people through the state, do not receive one shilling's advantage per annum, by reason of the great distance they live from the several schools, I think to annihilate all the Latin grammar schools, and establish one in a county, instead of the whole, will render more essential service to the community, and fix them on a more respectable footing than any plan which has as yet been suggested.
>
> My idea of the matter is simply this, that there should be a publick [sic] grammar school erected in each county, through this state, in which shall be taught, *English grammar, Latin, Greek, rhetoric, geography, mathematics, &c.* in order to fit young gentlemen for college, and school keeping. At the head of this county school, or academy, I would place an able preceptor, who should superintend the whole instruction of youth committed to his care; and who, together with a board of overseers, should annually examine young gentlemen designed for school matters, in *reading, writing, arithmetic, and English grammar;* and if found

qualified for the office of school keeping, and able to teach these branches with ease and propriety, to recommend them as such. But, with respect to those who are to enter college, a recommendation from the preceptor is sufficient. No man ought to be suffered to superintend ever so small a school, except he has been first examined by a body of men of this character, and authorized for that purpose, or had a degree at college or university. And, I am sure it is no vanity in me to think, that were our petty grammar schools annihilated, and one established in each county, as a substitute; and instead of common mock schools, kept by a set of *ignoramuses,* who obtrude themselves upon the people, a few months at a time, for no other reasons than to serve their own selfish purposes, without the requisite abilities of qualifications, we could have an amiable, worthy class of men, regularly introduced and examined as above mentioned, we should see the happy effects resulting from this noble plan. ([Friend of Liberty] 382 n, emphasis in original)

Several points in this passage are worth attention because they set the themes that are regularly repeated in the discussions of educating teachers. Notice in the first paragraph that the motivation for the new county schools is, at least in part, the economic inequality of requiring a community to support a school that does not benefit all the children of the community. Equality of opportunity, especially when the funding is supplied by taxes, is an essential feature of American democratic tradition. And, public education is a key component of ensuring the meritocracy that is so much a part of American cultural identity. Grammar schools, a level higher than the common schools, served only the most elite students of a community, young men of the best families who could do without the labor of these preadolescents. Grammar schools emphasized the studies, especially Latin, necessary for admittance to colonial colleges. Friend of Liberty's proposal is to change these schools in a way that "will render more essential service to the community." This new kind of school—"a publick [sic] grammar school"—would continue to prepare young men for college, but would also provide an advanced education for others so that they might become teachers in the common schools. The proposal, then, immediately recognizes the necessity of preparing teachers through advanced study, of making them "fit" for school keeping. Inherent in this suggestion, and the logic for including it in an essay in support of common schools, is a recognition of the need to create a larger teaching force to staff the proposed expansion of common school education.

Second, notice that there is a difference in the courses these "publick [sic] grammar schools" would offer and in the content knowledge on which students would be tested to be "found qualified for the office of school keeping." Students "designed for school matters" would evidently not be required to know Latin, Greek, rhetoric, or geography and only those portions of "mathematics" that could be said to be the same as "arithmetic." While the author does not explicitly state that the common grammar schools would contain two tracks—one for teachers and one for the college bound—it is not difficult to see how different curricula for different purposes are being superimposed on the different classes of students who would come together in this new community school. These class distinctions are further underscored in the closing lines of the footnote, where the author asserts that the method he is proposing will soon produce "an amiable, worthy class of men."

That the prospective teachers would be held responsible for fewer courses is less significant, however, than that the omitted courses were regarded as more rigorous and thus more prestigious. To know Latin and Greek at this time was a sign of upper-class status and to be trained in rhetoric was an indication of one's suitability for public speaking, and thus for public, political, and moral leadership. Embedded in this apparently simple list of standards for prospective teachers are assumptions about who would most likely choose school keeping as an occupation once it broadened to include those who were not clergy waiting for permanent appointments.

As explained in the first chapter, Roger Kimball's study of the use of the term *professional* and its relationship to cultural ideals establishes that in the colonial era when clergy were considered the most outstanding citizens, professionals were those men ordained to speak publicly (from the pulpit) and to serve the community selflessly. Junior clergy, waiting for an assignment to their own church, or those clergy who could not speak effectively from the pulpit, served as schoolteachers. Thus, even before the common school movement increased the demand for teachers and necessitated women entering the classroom, those who taught were considered either apprentices waiting for something better or inferiors who could do little else. Such devaluing of teaching is perpetuated in Friend of Liberty's 1789 public argument for the special preparation and testing of teachers, since the rhetorical education that might prepare teachers to participate in a more public domain or to assume the status of a professional has been precluded.

In Friend of Liberty's proposal, students who proceed to college would not be tested, but merely "recommended by the preceptor." On the surface, such a proposal may seem to hold prospective teachers to a higher standard. However, once finished with college, this nontested student could be hired to teach without undergoing any assessment of his qualifications to do so; having received a "recommendation" for advancing to the college level, the nontested student would be certified capable of teaching by virtue of having attended an institution of higher education. Thus, this early proposal for testing teachers before certifying them fit to keep school did not challenge the assumed relationship between knowledge and teaching, but offered an economical way to expand schools through the controlled employment of a lower class of men minimally prepared to be teachers. Opening school teaching to this lower class and preserving the possibility for college-educated men to also teach school did not transfer the status of the college men to teaching; in fact, by the second half of the nineteenth century, the concern would be how to attract college men into education when it paid so little and was held in such low regard. At some (perhaps unconscious) level, then, Friend of Liberty's proposal to expand teaching to a lower class and provide an alternative (read lesser) education to those who might become teachers is minor enough to be relegated to a footnote precisely because it builds on the already understood conception of teaching as inferior to other professions.

Notice, however, that the passage contains an interesting link between teaching and professional values. When the author claims that "instead of common mock schools, kept by a set of *ignoramuses*, who obtrude themselves upon the people, a few months at a time, for no other reasons than to serve their own selfish purposes," he links the teachers produced by his alternative plan to the opposite qualities. In other words, his plan would produce teachers who would be smart, unobtrusive, full-time, and who would act in service to others rather than in their own interests. These traits were already associated with professionals and would become even more so as the nineteenth century solidified the expectations for men to choose careers rather than simply work at one or more occupations. Although the author does not use the term *professional*—a conjugate Kimball has shown was not in widespread use until 1780–1830 when the legal profession assumed the preeminent position (139–45)—his construction of teaching as rightly done for selfless reasons is consistent with the then current conceptions of the learned professions. Perhaps again unintentionally, the author associates the traits of professionals with this new way of producing "a worthy class of men," and such rhetorical connections lay the groundwork for the expectation that school teaching would, indeed, be a profession. But the rhetoric of this passage also denies prospective teachers the intellectual preparation to assume the public profile of professionals. These deep contradictions arise in other examples as well.

Modern readers cannot help but notice the density of Friend of Liberty's prose: the abundance of commas and semicolons, the inverted subject/object word order, the notably unmodern way of using certain words. These features are, in some ways, easily dismissed as stylistic conventions of the time and genre; they are, we might believe, merely signs of the times. But the use of semicolons helps to link claims together without necessarily calling a reader's attention to how the link is made. Commas mark the numerous interrupting phrases, most often functioning as qualifiers and restrictions, but sometimes offering an aside, providing another name as an alternative, setting off items in a list, or separating introductory conjunctions from the sentence proper. Such constructions force a reader to pay close attention, or encourage jumping to the conclusion. In either case, the author is assumed to be reasoning carefully, building up the argument one deliberately wrought phrase at a time.

Likewise, the inverted word order draws attention away from the actors and toward the objects. In the sentence "No man ought to be suffered to superintend ever so small a school, except he has been first examined by a body of men of this character, and authorized for that purpose, or had a degree at college or university," for example, the first position is occupied by the men who will be tested, not by the men who will do the testing. In fact, the people who will examine the prospective teachers are not discussed. How they will be chosen, how they will know how to examine the candidate, how they will be "authorized" to perform this role, and who will do such authorizing is simply not stated. Thus, even the style of Friend of Liberty's proposal illustrates assumptions about the ease of determining a teacher's abilities, unarticulated connections between subject matter learning and suitability to teach, and control of schools and teachers by invisible members of a public community rather than by members of the profession.

The control of teachers by those who were not themselves teachers would become a source of controversy by 1837 when the attorney/businessperson/politician Horace Mann was appointed by the governor of Massachusetts to become the first Secretary of the State Board of Education over well-known schoolmen like James Carter (see Hinsdale 109–10, 181–209 for a complete description of this controversy). At the time of Friend of Liberty's proposal, however, the contradiction of having nonprofessionals certify teachers as fit for their jobs was not questionable enough to need elaboration or explanation. And, of course, teachers submitting themselves to some kind of community rather than professional examination or being evaluated on the achievements of their students continues even today.

To summarize, then, this earliest effort in America to suggest the need for educating teachers arose out of an argument for expanding common schooling to more students; it is a suggestion linked to economic arguments of fairness and equality in a democracy that was also clearly stratified by class. The curriculum for prospective teachers would be different, and less prestigious, than the instruction offered to students who would go on to advanced education and other professions. Testing would ensure the teachers' competency before they entered the profession, but instead of the profession of teachers controlling the testing (as entrance is controlled in other professions), outsiders—leaders in the community —would determine a teacher's competency. The plan for teaching teachers claims that teachers themselves would benefit by associating the qualities to be gained with professional status, but the curriculum and procedures outlined are clearly not marks of professionals. Finally, the style of making the proposal masks the contradictions embedded in the discourse. Because the author follows already accepted conceptions of teaching as a lesser occupation, the plan can be made to seem reasonable and can be asserted without elaborate substantiation in a footnote aside to the main argument about expanding common schooling.

Faulting Teachers, Contesting Teaching

By 1824, the assumption that better teachers would produce better schools had become the accusation that bad teaching was responsible for the problems in the public schools. But as this assumption/ accusation spawned public pleas for special schools, and thus funding, to prepare teachers before they entered the classroom, the implied definitions of teaching and the role of teachers began to show signs of cultural contestation. In other words, *teaching* as a key term began to have different meanings. In this section, I use a number of examples from the early public discussions of teacher education to illustrate both the shift from faulting schools to faulting teachers and the differences in the meaning of the term *teaching*.

Essays upon Popular Education with an Outline of an Institution for the Education of Teachers by the teacher/reformer and future legislator James Carter appeared first as a series published by the *Boston Patriot* in the winter of 1824–25. When it reappeared as a "widely and favorably" (American Council of Learned Societies "Carter" 538) reviewed book in 1826, it was advertised with this passage:

> Apart from the great faults in the government and instruction of the common schools, arising chiefly from the ignorance and inexperience of the teachers employed in them, many intelligent and patriotic citizens had come to regard with deep regret the course of legislation, in this state, upon the subject of popular education generally. (Carter iii)

Notice not only that the link between "faults . . . of the common schools" and the "ignorance and inexperience of teachers" become a cause-effect relationship but also that Carter can treat the connection as a commonplace by setting it off from the main clause as an interrupting verbal phrase. Criticism of teachers and arguments about the need for special schools to prepare teachers also begin to appear in government documents—like state resolutions and reports of legislative committees—as early as 1827, when the School Visitors Society in Connecticut passed a resolution that read:

> There are serious deficiencies and evils in the existing state of common schools, which may and ought to be remedied; that some of the prominent evils are incompetency in teachers, both as to literary attainments and the proper qualifications for instruction; the great variety and deficiency of school-books; the defective mode of examining teachers and visiting schools; and the shortness of time in which schools are taught. (Butler 376)

In the same year, the Select Committee of the House of Representatives of Massachusetts, which had been asked to make recommendations regarding a seminary for the instruction of schoolteachers, reported:

> It needs at this time neither argument, nor an exhibition of facts to demonstrate to the legislature, that the free schools of the commonwealth are not such as they ought to be—that they fail most essentially, of accomplishing the high objects for which they were established, and towards the support of which so large an amount of money is annually raised amongst the people. Upon this subject public opinion is fully settled. Nor is there any difficulty in arriving at the true cause. Can it, in the large majority of cases, be traced to any other than the incompetency of teachers? And in this fact there is nothing mysterious. Can the teachers be otherwise than incompetent, when no pains are taken to instruct them in the business of their profession—when, in one word, they are not reputed or constituted a profession? (Calhoun 155)

As is evident in these examples, writers regularly constructed the state of affairs as riddled with "evils," "faults," "deficiencies," and the like as they argued for legislative and public support for special schools to prepare teachers. As outlined in the first chapter, scholars of professionalization have identified one of the primary features necessary to the making of a profession as the construction of a "crisis" that can only continue to worsen unless the special skills and talents of the proposed profession are brought in to correct, cure, or otherwise eliminate the problem through their specialized knowledge (Ehrenreich). In this sense, the calls to professionalize teaching through the creation of teachers' seminaries, and eventually normal schools, are signs of the attempts to create a profession through the rhetorical construction of schools, and a nation, in trouble.

There is an important difference, however, between finding fault in the schools and laying the responsibilities for these failings firmly at the feet of the teachers then employed: schools are bureaucratic institutions belonging to the community at large, but teachers are individual bodies. Improving schools must require attention to material conditions, structures, and forces at work within the community that might be responsible for the shortcomings and that, if altered, might lead to improved results from these culturally controlled institutional structures. Improving teachers, however, requires attention to the individual bodies, minds, and souls of those who teach. If teachers and not schools are at fault, then the community's responsibility, and the necessity to respond with financial or material support, is lessened. If teachers and not school structures are the failure, then teachers who act, think, and/or believe differently from those who exist at present must be created. The possibility remains, however, that these new individuals will still not have the power to solve the problems or evils located in others who do the same job. Thus, the claim that the individual professional can correct the "evils" that have been identified is made suspect before that professional has even been created.

Creating such different-minded individuals suggests, however, at least three alternatives. First, individuals can be given a different kind of training from what they have been given previously. This alternative produces the argument for specialized schools to prepare teachers. Second, different kinds of individuals can be recruited into teaching, an alternative that generates the effort to expand the teaching force to include those who would not have previously been allowed to teach. Third, the definition of teaching can be altered so that something different from the previous activities and mind-set becomes the cultural expectation. Under this final alternative, teaching has to become something other than monitoring a natural and unproblematic transference of information or skill.

The link between educational failings, teachers, and professionalization continued in these public discussions, and the cultural contest over teaching can be seen from a later vantage point to be interspersed throughout the various arguments for professionalizing teaching. Making teaching into a profession given the lowered status with which it was already associated was no easy task, however. Those who thought most carefully about how teachers should be prepared did not always win the debate, and their own rhetorical choices were likely to employ contradictory definitions of teaching as well.

In the sixth essay in his series on public education, for example, Carter provides an outline for an institution for the education of teachers that includes a wide range of intellectual studies as well as opportunities to observe children learning. Carter lists the essentials of a teacher seminary as

- a library with books on science of education, on physical education, mental development, moral education and language;
- a principal and assistant professors of every branch;
- a school of children; and,
- a board of commissioners. (51–56)

These particulars clearly imply the different and specialized preparation to teach that differentiate Carter's plan from the preparation teachers would have previously received. Unlike Friend of Liberty's proposal that I examined earlier in this chapter, Carter is not merely listing areas of study that duplicate the subjects that would be taught in the common schools. Likewise, requiring a school of children as a part of the preparation suggests a role for observation, demonstration, practice, and experience that clearly was not a part of the preteaching experience of those who attended colleges and were hired as teachers during their vacations or before finding permanent employment. Attention to the learner rather than to only the subject matter marks an important shift in the conception of teaching. This shift, in fact, paved the way for women to be accepted as teachers, since women were thought to be more "naturally" inclined to attend to the needs of others. Despite these differences, however, Carter's list is still introduced with the familiar frame that implies flaws in the character of the individual teachers.

> [t]he character of the schools, and of course their political, moral, and religious influence upon the community, depend, almost solely, upon the character of the teachers.... So that whatever is done to elevate the character of teachers, elevates, at the same time, and in the same degree, the character of the schools which they teach, and enlarges and strengthens their influence upon the community. (43–44)

The issue of "character" was linked to the corrective supplied by professionalizing when Carter claims:

> [i]t would be a natural result of the proposed institution, to organize the teachers into a more distinct profession, and to raise the general standard of their intellectual attainments. (59)

Thus, Carter's argument for a teacher seminary, despite its emphasis on the specialized intellectual preparation teachers needed, arises from the language of blame and assumes unquestioningly the necessity of a particular kind of character and the power of professionalization to instill these appropriate values. Indeed, the very naming of this preparatory school a "seminary" suggests the need to instill values and behaviors associated with the calling to be a professional, values and behaviors that would have been connected more commonly with the elite education of colonial-era colleges than would the expertise of specialized study.

The point is not that Carter was simply speaking out of both sides of his mouth or that he was employing whatever arguments he thought might be persuasive to the Boston public at that moment. Instead, such internal contradictions in language and argument seem indicative of moments when cultural values and forms are undergoing transformation and thus moments when meanings of key terms are being contested. In this case, the cultural values of education are clearly in transition as schools expand to accommodate increasing numbers of students and increasing literacy expectations, and so the prior meaning of teacher as one who is unable to assume the public role of the ministry or is in waiting for such a position is in conflict with a meaning that draws on the special expertise and education of a professional. Teaching is being redefined as a profession in which attention to the learner is as important as attention to the subject matter.

This contesting of cultural meanings is evident in other arguments about teacher preparation as well. For example, in the same year that Carter made his case to the Boston public, 1824–25, Walter R. Johnson, the principal of the Academy at Germantown, published a pamphlet entitled "Observations on the Improvement of Seminaries of Learning in the United States: with Suggestions for its Accomplishment." Johnson began his suggestions for improvement just as Carter did, with a statement about the current conditions of schools and the need for better teachers.

> It is believed that the demand for good instructors is increasing in our country, in a ratio far exceeding that of the augmentation of our population. This belief is founded upon the consideration that many of the States, which have hitherto been destitute of school systems, are now forming plans for the general or universal diffusion of knowledge: that higher institutions, as well as common schools, are in all parts of the Union becoming the objects of favor and attention, to a degree heretofore unequaled: that in seminaries of every grade, the number of branches expected to be taught, is much greater than formerly: that in every quarter it is beginning to be understood, that under free political institutions, the cause of good learning is the foundation of success to all other good causes, and that as the public become enlightened on the subject, they are also becoming better qualified to distinguish the able from the imbecile, and those who act from principle from those who follow caprice or sordid interest alone. It is daily made more and more evident, even to those who reflect but little, that every man is not by nature an instructor; a truth which seems to have been overlooked by those who have

been ready to employ the weak, untaught, and inexperienced for those offices of the utmost importance. Besides, the qualifications of instructors must bear some proportion to the attainments required by their pupils in after life, by the circumstances in which they are to be placed. (799–800)

Johnson's claim that the demand for "good instructors" is increasing more than growth in population alone can account for is based on a two-prong argument. In the first half of the previous quotation, he establishes that there is an increased demand in both the number of schools and the subjects being taught. He then argues that the public has become better able to judge the quality of individual teachers both by their principled actions and by the relative success of their students. Each of these links—to the job market and to what we now call "teacher accountability" based on evidence of students' success—has continued to be a part of the discussions about professionalizing teaching and improving schools by improving (or monitoring) teachers; each has continued to be a standard solution to educational problems. Notice also that Johnson connects good teaching with the values associated with professionals who "act from principle(s)" that they have learned to apply to the specifics of individual cases and who do not "follow caprice or sordid interest alone," but observe good practice as defined by the profession serving the public rather than themselves.

Johnson was, like Carter, also interested in enhancing the professional status of teaching itself, and by institutionalizing and systematizing the preparation to teach, Johnson assumed that teaching would become like other professions:

> we ought, perhaps, . . . to think it remarkable that it has not been done sooner: that while every other profession has its appropriate schools for preparation, *that* on which the usefulness and respectability of all others essentially depend, is left to the will of chance, or *"to take care of itself."* We have theological seminaries—law schools—medical

colleges—military academies—institutes for mechanics—and colleges of pharmacy for apothecaries; but no shadow of an appropriate institution to qualify persons for discharging with ability and success, the duties of *instruction,* either in these professional seminaries, or in any other. Men have been apparently presumed to be qualified to *teach,* from the moment that they passed the period of ordinary pupil-age; a supposition which, with a few exceptions, must, of course, lead only to disappointment and mortification. It has often been asked why men will not devote themselves *permanently* to the profession of teaching. Among other reasons, much weight is, no doubt, to be attached to this want of preparation, and to the discouragements and perplexities encountered in blindly attempting to hit upon the right course of procedure. (800, emphasis in original)

And, like Carter, Johnson provides a sketch of what he believes is essential to the preparation of teachers.

The practice of superintending, of arranging into classes, instructing and governing, ought to form *one* part of the duty of the young teacher. The attending of lectures on the science of mental development, and the various collateral topics, should constitute another. An extensive course of reading and study of authors who have written with ability and practical good sense on the subject, would be necessary, in order to expahd the mind, and free it from those prejudices which, on this subject, are apt to adhere even to persons who fancy themselves farthest removed from their influence. (801, emphasis in original)

The emphasis Johnson puts on what we would now call "classroom management" being only *"one"* part of what teachers would need to do and know is significant. What takes precedence for Johnson is the reading and study of "mental development and the various collateral topics" that "expand the mind." In addition to learning the scholarship of education, removing prejudices, and, we can suppose, coming to share the particular beliefs and practices of a *profession,* Johnson's preparation to teach has at its core the expanded intellectual capability of the teacher in ways that are, again, not limited to simply knowing the content material to be taught. In other words, implicit in this view of professional preparation is an ideology and an epistemology that is in opposition to the view that teaching is simply knowledge transfer, that any college graduate could be a teacher or that teachers need not have the same characteristics as other professionals. Even if neither the ideology nor the epistemology is overtly argued to the public being persuaded that teacher training is necessary, even if neither is completely visible to the would-be teachers who were to submit themselves to such training, their presence is detectable in these documents.

Johnson's recognition that "the qualifications of instructors must bear some proportion to the attainments required by their pupils in after life" suggests that he imagines different levels of teachers for different levels or kinds of students. Although such a conception of the profession of teaching may be appropriate, it also allows for the hierarchy that transfers the (lower) prestige of students to their teachers. Thus teachers of the young, the poor, or the less able become by association lesser as well. Such language also implies that the evaluation of teachers is bound to the "products" they produce: their students. Making students the measure of teaching success not only further paved the way for a conception of teaching as service and care but also added an additional external (rather than professional) evaluator.

Likewise, Johnson obscures the other reasons that might lead men to refuse to "devote themselves *permanently* to the profession of teaching," including such material conditions as low pay, lack of prestige, limited autonomy, or overcrowded and inadequately supplied classrooms. While these other reasons have been forced into the shadows by Johnson's rhetorical choices, they are nevertheless present to readers aware of the conditions of schools. The use of italics to underscore key terms—*instruction, teach, permanently—*

works as a contrast to the definition Johnson is arguing against *that* (which will) *"take care of itself."*

Thus, embedded in both of these public arguments of the early 1800s are traces of contested conceptions of teaching and rhetorical constructions that provide insight to the cultural assumptions about teachers. Those assumptions include that individual teachers rather than economic conditions or institutional structures are to blame for the failings of schools; that these teachers can be improved through a program of professionalization that includes specialized study and instilling values associated with the elite who are already able to be professionals, values that include attention and service to the client who is the student; that democratic meritocracy can be achieved through schooling; and that good teaching can be measured by the degree of success students in the democratic meritocracy are able to achieve. The attempt to redefine teaching and to transform teachers into professionals, however, is made more difficult by these very assumptions.

In 1832, Samuel Reed Hall, a Congregationalist minister, published *Lectures on School-Keeping,* the first such publication in either Britain or the United States. Hall's text also begins with the link between faults in the schools and the poor preparation of teachers:

> There is a very general belief, that one of the most common defects is the improper character and superficial qualifications of teachers. It is well known that many who are employed to teach our primary schools, are deficient in almost every necessary qualification. While this defect is so prominent, all the efforts to increase the usefulness of schools, can be attended with only partial success. But let the character of the teachers be improved, and improvement in schools will follow of course. To accomplish this object, it is desirable that institutions should be established for educating teachers, where they should be taught not only the necessary branches of literature, but, be made acquainted with the science of *teaching* and the mode of *governing* a school with success. The general management of a

school should be a subject of *much study*, before one engages in the employment of teaching. (iii–iv, emphasis in original)

Although Hall uses the language of "character" as is typical of this time period (Cohen 92–99), he clearly means for teachers to have much more than good morals or ethical behavior. His lectures list qualifications of teachers as

- common sense, including observation, judgment, discrimination, reason, not passion or prejudice;
- uniformity of temper;
- capacity to understand and discriminate character;
- convictions;
- affection;
- moral discernment; and,
- literary knowledge including reading, writing, grammar, arithmetic, geography, U.S. history, science, spelling, and vocabulary. (31–42)

These characteristics are essentially the same as the traits associated with *professional*, absent, of course, the capacity to assume a public leadership role through the ability to speak from the pulpit, in court, or in a legislative chamber. Reinforced in Hall's list, even in its order and elaboration, is the attention to the student as client and the ethic of care evidenced in Carter's and Johnson's texts of the same period. Hall also urges teachers to "become acquainted with the nature of your employment" by reading on the subject in professional journals like the *Journal of Education* and *The School Magazine,* by observing children and parents, by conversing with other teachers, and by "consider[ing] the responsibility of the station you are to occupy" (48). Thus, like Johnson and Carter, Hall uses language that reimagines teachers as both intelligent and (almost) professional even while he faults teachers rather than the structures within which they had to work. Though Hall does not use the term *professional,* he does imagine a specific course of study that includes "the *science* of teaching," and so, like other advocates of specialized preparation to teach, his definition of teaching requires advanced knowledge that would make the teacher qualified as an expert and not merely a knower of content information. But, again like Carter and Johnson, Hall's text demonstrates the contradictions of this moment of cultural contestation when it includes a separate essay directed at female teachers. Even though Hall insists that female teachers—who would, he imagines, work only with the very young—need the same training as other teachers, the separation of women teachers into a narrower range of teaching opportunities suggests a profession that was already becoming highly gendered. Before I examine how the gendering of teaching further contradicted the redefining of teaching as a profession, however, I turn to the evidence of what early teacher educators like Hall were actually able to put into practice to see the patterns of contested meanings more clearly.

Teaching Teachers

No one disputes that the number of schools and students increased throughout the nineteenth century, nor that the pressure of numbers largely prohibited the careful and thorough preparation of all teachers that Carter, Johnson, and Hall imagined. Before the publication of his book on school-keeping, Hall opened what is credited as the first school for teacher training in the United States. Begun in 1823 in Concord, Vermont, Hall's Concord Academy enrolled 224 boys and girls in the first three years, though most attended for only a single term. In 1830, Hall transferred to Andover Seminary to begin a teacher's department with a three-year course of study. Students at Andover were required to take entrance exams in English, spelling, geography, and arithmetic. Hall's efforts to establish teacher seminaries were not, however, financially successful. His last and most complex attempt was a school in Plymouth, New Hampshire, that began with eight teachers in addition to Hall and 248 students, 110 of them female. This seminary required four years of study for men and three for women, with four terms in each academic year. Students were permitted to be absent from the seminary one term each year in order to teach school, perhaps to earn the funds they would need for further schooling, perhaps as a less expensive alternative for gaining practical experience than having a model or demonstration school as a part of the seminary itself. In any case, Hall's Plymouth school folded because of financial problems in less than three years, not even enough time to graduate a student from the female department (Wright 18–26).

The first state-supported normal schools began in Massachusetts in 1839, though New York had been offering some state funds to private seminaries for teachers as early as 1834 (Elsbree 146). The financial pressures were felt by the states just as they were by private institutions like Hall's. In 1841, for example, the Massachusetts legislature debated, but eventually defeated, legislation that would have eliminated public funding for normal schools as an unnecessary expense (Butler 300). Early professional organizations like the American Institute of Instruction passed resolutions in support of seminaries for teachers, and their conferences included discussions of what those seminaries ought to require. However, it took until well after the Civil War for normal schools to become common even in the heavily populated Northeast, and it was not until the end of the century that professional training for teachers had become expected. Kimball gives these figures: there were 19 normal schools nationwide just before the Civil War; 139 by 1876; 242 by 1892; and 362 public and private normal schools by 1900, along with 929 high schools and academies offering professional courses for teaching by the same year (250).

Even with this growth, Elsbree estimates the number of new teachers needed to staff elementary schools in 1897–98 was four and half times the number prepared by public and private normal schools (314). Massachusetts, one of the states with the oldest commitment to public normal schools, for example, reported that only 38.5 percent of its teachers in 1897–98 had any normal school training, and only 33.5 percent were normal school graduates (Elsbree 314). In 1901, Frank L. Jones, the superintendent of education for the state of Indiana, reported to the National Education Association (NEA) on a survey of teachers in ten northern states that 2,450 (nearly 12 percent) of a total of 20,662 teachers were "teaching without previous experience, 4,880 (23.6 percent) had only a common school education, and 8,600 (41.6 percent) had not studied beyond the high school" (Kirkland 252–53). Given how much longer universal schooling and normal schools had been in operation in the North, it was certainly no surprise that the southern states were even further behind at this point; Dr. J. H. Kirkland, the chancellor of Vanderbilt University, reported that of 9,396 certificates issued in 1900 in Tennessee, 7,086 were the lowest level, "third grade," indicating less than high school graduation, and "few, if any, of these teachers had had any instruction in school methods" (Kirkland 254).

Because normal schools through most of the century needed students in order to stay financially solvent, they often admitted applicants who needed considerable basic instruction before beginning the more professional studies. Cyrus Peirce—the son of a prominent Massachusetts family, a graduate of Harvard College and Harvard Divinity School, and a Congregational minister who found himself more successful in the schoolroom than in the pulpit—was unanimously elected by the state school board to be the principal of Massachusetts's first normal school in 1839 (American Council of Learned Societies "Peirce" 404). His diary records his impressions of the abilities and progress of his first students:

> Aug. 27: I think the scholars have not been much habituated to hard close and methodical studying. There is great deficiency among them in knowledge of the Common Branches. With two or three exceptions, most that are in school I think will need nearly all the first year to fit themselves thoroughly. Reading, Spelling, Grammar, Arithmetic, Geography all need attention.
>
> Sept. 9: They seem industrious and interested; and nearly every one of *fair* capacity. But many of them are yet backward; and I apprehend it will require more than one year's Instruction to qualify them to teach. They want language—they want the power of generalization, and of communication.
>
> Sept. 21: Most of the pupils need most of their time for

the common Branches—There is great deficiency in Reading and Spelling.

Oct. 1: Few of them think of staying more than one year; all of which with great diligence, will be required to prepare them to teach in the *Common* Branches. (1329–31, emphasis in original)

Reading this diary makes it clear that Peirce believed that the necessity of providing basic instruction to prospective teachers left little time for more advanced study of pedagogy or child development. There was, then, a hierarchy for Peirce that required prospective teachers to have mastered the common school subjects before undertaking the specialized study that would make them professionals. Thus, the rhetorical arguments for a different preparation of teachers—a preparation that was to have done more than teach the common school subjects—were not substantiated by real practices. That the students who attended these normal schools had little prior schooling is clear; unspoken here is the material differences in class standing that accounted for those deficiencies.

Still, Peirce is known for supporting "learning by doing," and his diary also includes notes about having his students experiment with barometers, thermometers, suction and forcing pumps, activities that would have demonstrated a definition of teaching as something other than direct transference of knowledge. Furthermore, Peirce was among the early advocates of including a demonstration school as part of the normal school curriculum, a feature that existed only in the normal school at Framingham until mandated by the state in 1896 (Holmes and Weiss). Thus, coexisting with what these early teacher educators perceived as the glaring need to provide future teachers a level of basic schooling were their conceptualizations of a different definition of teaching and thus of teacher preparation —a more professional education—centered on how learning happened rather than on the subjects to be learned.

In fact, principals of normal schools and members of professional organizations argued about the appropriate kinds of instruction, admission qualifications, and the balance between basic instruction and opportunities for practice in teaching throughout the nineteenth century. Such debates reflect, of course, the tensions that arise as conceptions of education change and as the terms that name those concepts are given different meanings. As the educational historian Sol Cohen has suggested, the shifts in discourse that mark the transformation of schools generally associated with "progressive" education did not happen all at once, but gradually over time, and individuals did not consistently speak either the language of conservation or the language of progression. Thus, in these early discussions of the kinds of preparation that teachers should receive, we can trace both meanings of *teaching*: an older meaning of the unproblematic transmission of knowledge and a newer meaning that employs a progressive language of child development, learning by doing, and inquiry. Likewise, it is possible to see the emphasis on "common branches" of learning and the "want of language" as signs that Peirce's students were indeed members of a less cultured class or merely that Peirce conceived of his role as primarily instilling the values that would then be inculcated into the children of the common schools.

Whatever the reason for normal schools spending so much time teaching these common branches, the increased schooling for those who would be teachers certainly did not translate into an increase in status for teachers. In fact, just the contrary. Button and Provenzo argue that as schooling expanded and classical study came to be less important, "master" as the term to name the instructor was replaced by "teacher" (95–98). At the same time, the number of female teachers increased dramatically. By 1842, the number of female teachers in New England was nearly twice the number of male teachers. Butler gives the figures as 4,112 women and 2,491 male teachers for 3,103 schools that enrolled 155,041 children (302). The percentage of male teachers continued to drop throughout the century, though exactly when the shift to primarily female teachers happened varied by region, as is evident in the statistics in table 2.1.

The disproportionate number of women teachers existed, in part, because school districts paid women about one-third what they paid their male counterparts; according to Butler, pay rates for women averaged $12.81 per month, compared to $33.80 per month

Table 2.1 Percentage of Male Teachers in State School Systems

	1870–71	1879–80	1889–90	1893–94
North Atlantic	26.2	28.8	20.0	19.0
South Atlantic	63.8	62.5	49.1	45.1
South Central	67.5	67.2	57.5	53.7
North Central	43.3	41.7	32.4	29.4
Western	45.0	40.3	31.1	29.6

Source: Bureau of Education 15.

for men, and the school year lasted slightly more than seven months (302). The pay differential further increased the trend toward the feminization of teaching, and the low salaries were recognized as an obstacle both to attracting better teachers and to having teaching recognized as a profession.

These material conditions are important to the consideration of the rhetorical constructions of teaching. Because teaching was being redefined as more centered on the learner than on the subject matter at the same time that women were entering classrooms in increasing numbers, the shift in definition would inevitably be associated with the shift in gender as well, even if the actual practices of these teacher seminaries did not, in fact, alter the emphasis on subject matter study. While alternative names for this classroom role like "master" were being eliminated because of their association with men, the remaining term—"teacher"—would become even more firmly tied to women.

Gendering Teaching

Of course, women could not have entered teaching without a shift in cultural expectations that permitted them to assume jobs outside the home. Catherine Beecher is credited with advancing the argument that teaching was an appropriate occupation for women because it required the same skills associated with mothering, and these early teacher educators clearly imagined that female teachers would work only with the youngest children, and only until they married and had children of their own. The feminization of teaching allowed the problems in staffing the increased number of schools to be solved without undue expense to communities, because women could be paid so much less than men could. Beecher also anticipated a method of professionalizing education by creating a hierarchy in which principals would supervise the less prepared classroom teacher. In her 1829 *Suggestions Respecting Improvements in Education,* Beecher argues that:

> Whatever be the qualifications of the teachers in each department, the *care* of each must, in a greater or less degree, fall upon the principal. What books shall be used, what mode of instruction adopted, what facilities for illustration procured, how much time and attention each teacher may claim from their several pupils without interfering with the claims of the others, all these particulars must be submitted to the person who has a general knowledge of the interests of the whole. . . . There must be one mind to superintend in the other departments of education, as much as in the literary and scientific. To these objects there must be the energies of one mind devoted, and making all other things secondary, just as in each of the branches of instruction there is a teacher who makes intellectual culture the primary object of attention, and other things but secondary. It is true every teacher must *aid,* but there must be one directing mind; one whose business it is to devise plans for others to execute, and to see that nothing is left unattempted in these more than in other departments. And none but a *principal* can take such a station in this institution, as would be very apparent to any person who knows intimately its concerns. (62, 67, emphasis in original)

In this passage, Beecher distinguishes the curricular and pedagogical decisions that must be made from the attention that is given to the "intellectual culture" of each branch of study, whether literary or scientific. Nevertheless, she describes these departments or activities of "education" as needing the "energies" and "devotion" of the "mind." Notice, however, that the mind that considers such choices as "what books shall be used, what mode of instruction adopted, what facilities for illustration procured, how much time and attention each teacher may claim from their several pupils without interfering with the claims of the others" is not the classroom teacher who is responsible for "execut[ing]" the plans made by the one "directing mind."

Beecher, of course, imagined that women would hold even these principalships, since, in her view, women were "naturally" suited for the work of educating the young. But her rhetoric linked classroom teachers to the nonprofessional activities of "mothering," a natural ability of any female, and the decision making and oversight role of the principal—the intellectual activity of the "directing mind"—could thus be easily attributed as more "naturally" male. By the end of the nineteenth century, offering men the supervising roles over classroom teachers helped to attract more men into the profession and provided them with higher salaries at the expense of the mostly female teaching staff, a pattern of professionalizing education well established by scholars like Apple and Stober and Tyack, and one that I return to in the fourth chapter.

The separation of the decision making from the execution of the curriculum continued throughout the nineteenth century and was reinforced by assumptions about the intellectual capacity of women and their natural abilities to care for and nurture others, even as the percentage of women in the classroom grew and the grade levels they were allowed to teach expanded. Likewise, even when the majority of classrooms contained female teachers, professional organizations resisted including them as full members of the profession. Female teachers were routinely invited to attend educational conferences, but they were not always allowed to become members of the organization.

The American Institute of Instruction, for example, the first organization for those involved in education, was formed in 1830, but it did not allow women to become members until 1868. The participation of women as guest speakers was also limited, as the minutes of the 1834 session demonstrate. In that year, Mr. Alcott of Germantown brought an essay on Moral Instruction written by Miss Robbins of Hartford before the board of directors and asked that it be presented. The matter was referred to the censors "to be disposed of at their discretion" (Board of Censors xviii). Another essay by Mrs. Hayward of South Boston was treated similarly, but there is no notation of how the censors "disposed" of these essays by women.

It was not until 1850 that an essay written by a woman, Elizabeth Peabody's "Essay on History," was read before the institute's convention. Though Peabody was acknowledged as the author, a male member read the essay aloud after it had been reviewed and approved by a committee of men (Board of Censors x–xii). The essay did not, however, get chosen as one of the ones printed by the institute in its annual proceedings. In fact, it was not until 1875 that a woman's essay—Anna C. Brackett's "Doctors and Teachers: The Relation of the Medical and Educational Professions"—appeared in the printed record of the institute. Brackett was not, however, merely a classroom teacher; she had been a principal of normal schools in Charleston and St. Louis and was the founder and principal of a highly respected private school for girls in New York City at the time of her address to the institute. She was fluent in German and so knew firsthand the works of the German philosophers influencing American education, and she published a translation of Rosenkranz's educational philosophy for the International Educational Series edited by William T. Harris, the commissioner of education (American Council of Learned Societies "Brackett" 546–47). Thus, it is difficult to know if the change in the institute's practice was a sign of increased regard for female educators in general or a continuation of the privileging of "masters" over "teachers."

Even the more limited role of participating in discussions was apparently denied to females in the audience at the convention, at least in the earliest years of the organization. An 1840 resolution to "permit teachers, male and female, in attendance to express experience in teaching and governing schools" (Board of Censors ix–x) was discussed, but was indefinitely postponed, and subsequent proceedings do not record any action on the resolution. Since discussion is recorded inconsistently, it is difficult to know when women began to contribute to the open discussions, if they ever did. By the time the constitution was changed in 1868 to allow any "person" involved in schools to become a member of the organization rather than any "gentleman," (101) the issue was not controversial enough to receive any recorded discussion, but that does not mean that women were treated as equal members of the profession from then on. In 1869, only two women are recorded as assuming any official duties, and those two—Josephine Ellery of Gloucester, Massachusetts, and a Miss Perkins of Bath, Maine—served in the relatively minor role of members of the Committee on Resolutions (10). Women did not begin to serve on the board of directors of the organization until 1877.

Although such overt denial of the right of female teachers to participate in this professional organization supports an interpretation that the public speaking associated with professionalism kept women from gaining professional status, the evidence is not as clear cut as it might appear from examining only the American Institute of Instruction. The NEA, founded in 1857 as the National Teachers Association, for example, changed its constitution to allow women members in 1866 (Lieberman 260). The NEA also included women as speakers, members of committees, and participants in discussions even though they did not have a woman president until Ella Flagg Young, the superintendent of schools in Chicago, was elected in 1910. Given the preponderance of women in most of the nation's classrooms by midcentury, however, it is clear that, even in the NEA, the percentage of women who were visible professionally was much lower than the percentage of men. And, the women who did participate in these early years were principals of normal schools, college-educated high school teachers, or founders of women's academies; in other words, they were women who already had more status than the majority of classroom teachers.

Of the 378 listed NEA members for 1873, for example, 112 (nearly 30 percent) of them can be identified as women on the basis of unambiguous first names, but only four women are recorded as serving on the twenty-seven-member nominating committee, no women are listed as presenters at any of the general sessions that year, and only two women are recorded as having presented papers to the smaller gatherings of departments. This pattern of limited participation continues throughout the nineteenth century, with women apparently most active in the departments of elementary schools and normal schools. Can it be only a coincidence that when the NEA held its annual meeting in conjunction with the American Institute of Instruction in 1882, no women presented papers even in the departments?

Similarly, should we think it insignificant that at the 1893 convention held as a special session of the International Congress of Education as a part of the World's Columbian Exposition in Chicago, women were again included in limited roles? In three consecutive evenings of general sessions, only one woman, Miss E. P. Hughes, presented a paper or led a discussion. Hughes's paper, "The Professional Training of Teachers for Secondary Schools," does not appear in the published proceedings with the other keynote presentations, but is placed with the papers presented to the meetings of the Secondary Schools Departments. The distribution of papers/discussions at these individual departments is also suggestive (see table 2.2).

While the division of education into these different departments is an interesting indication of the conception of the profession at the time, the interest here is in the relative status afforded women within the professional organizations. Clearly, the domain of the female teacher was much more narrowly proscribed than it was for men at that time. And, while it might be "natural" that women would not present at the departments of technological and industrial instruction, it seems antithetical for women to have had such a small role within the elementary department when their numbers in elementary classrooms were so large. Michael Apple provides statistics for 1890, for example, listing the number of females teaching in public elementary schools as 232,925, compared to 121,877 men, so 65.6 percent of elementary teachers were female three years before the Columbian Exposition (460). Likewise, given the expectation for women (at least middle- and upper-class

Table 2.2 Presenters of Papers at the 1893 International Congress of Education, World's Columbian Exposition, in Chicago, by Gender and NEA Department

Department	Men	Women
School supervision	5	1
Secondary schools	8	3
Higher education	12	0
Elementary schools	17	2
Kindergarten	3	11
Prof. training of teachers	16	2
Art	7	4
Vocal music	4	0
Technological instruction	9	0
Industrial instruction	6	0
Physical education	13	1 (discussion only)
Rational psychology	6	0
Experiential psychology	12	3
Business education	7	1
Educational publications	12	0

Note: NEA = National Education Association, Prof. = professional.

women) to be well trained in art and music, it seems extraordinary that these divisions would not have had more women participants.

Another oddity visible in the journal proceedings of the 1893 convention is an appendix of fourteen papers, eleven written by women, on the theme "The Education of Women in Great Britain and her Colonies." William T. Harris, who as commissioner of education chaired the committee in charge of the International Congress of Education for the Columbian Exposition, apparently solicited the papers by suggesting the topic to Millicent Garrett Fawcett, who oversaw their production. The papers were not delivered at the congress, however, but the NEA included them as an appendix to its journal proceedings without further explanation.

Such a contradiction of creating a special venue for a focus on women and simultaneously denying their full participation was, according to the cultural historian Reid Badger, a reoccurring feature of the Columbian Exposition, and of American culture more generally, at the end of the nineteenth century. As Badger explains in his history of the exposition, the symbolic confusion of American culture is well represented by the exposition's treatment of women (120–23). Women were given a prominence in exhibits with their own building, special congresses, and a dormitory to encourage attendance by working women. Moreover, women were included in the administrative planning of the exposition through the special Board of Lady Managers. But the representations of women juxtaposed the Victorian idealized woman of purity with "Algerian and Egyptian girls performing suggestive dances" on the midway (Badger 121). Likewise, the stated aim of the women's exhibits was to "break down the older view of woman's work and woman's place," but most of the exhibits actually "focused on traditional areas of child rearing, education, the 'divine art of healing,' and cooking" (Badger 121). Badger thus concludes, "Taken as a whole then, the World's Columbian Exposition offered a conflicting picture of the American woman"; it gave "women more public attention than ever before and provided opportunities for them to participate more fully in such an important national enterprise, [but] it did not thereby announce a revolution" (122).

The contest over teaching—which by the end of the nineteenth century had become thoroughly feminized—repeats some of the paradoxes visible in the changing conceptions of woman that circulated at the same time. Indeed, the various obstacles to women gaining full professional standing can be understood as part of what Barbara Harris's study of women and the professions argues was a long-standing conception of women's abilities inherited from Europe and overlaid by Victorian values. Throughout the nineteenth century, Harris demonstrates, cultural values made it difficult for women to leave the home to pursue professional work unless that work was considered in keeping with the "cult of domesticity." Since caring for children was an appropriate "female" task, teaching was the first occupation to admit women wishing to work outside the home, followed fairly quickly by nursing and social work. The Civil

War, Harris argues, allowed more women to enter the workplace, and the lack of male students forced more colleges to admit women in order to stay financially solvent, but even with these advancements, only 25.2 percent of American women were working by 1910, and the majority of these were immigrants. By 1920, only 11.9 percent of the women working were in the professions, and 75 percent of these were in teaching or nursing. As early as 1920, half of college students were women, and one-third of the graduate degrees were awarded to women, but less than 8 percent of the college professors, barely 3 percent of the lawyers, and smaller percentages of doctors and ministers were women (104–5, 117). Harris concludes from this data that even as women gained education, they did not secure jobs, a serious contradiction to the American belief in meritocracy through education.

Carter and Prus argue, however, that access to jobs for women at the end of the nineteenth century was gained almost entirely through schooling, rather than the multiple venues available to men, so it is logical that even high school attendance rates would be higher for women than for men. According to Carter and Prus, the pay scale for women in industry at that time ranged from $3.50 to $6.50 per week (with few earning the upper end), and the pay scale for female teachers averaged $9.73 per week. With such a marked difference in economic benefit, teaching must have been seen as a very attractive alternative to factory work even though women earned considerably less than their male colleagues did.

Thus, whether we look at the arguments for permitting women into teaching, their inclusion in professional organizations, or the statistics about their employment and rates of pay, the pattern of women in classrooms (where men generally were not) and their absence from leadership positions (where men dominated) seems clear enough. Teaching might be redefined as centered on the learner rather than the subject matter, but such a construction only further cemented the feminization of teaching precisely because attention to students could be equated to the "natural" female role of mothering. Complicating this picture, of course, is the evidence that lower-class students were able to use schooling and teaching as a means of upward mobility, but this factor, too, contributed to the lack of professional status for teaching.

For example, shortly after the Civil War, a residence hall was created at the Public Normal School at Framingham, Massachusetts, because most students at the time could not afford the expense of lodging in town (Holmes and Weiss 56). There is also evidence that the school began to admit more minority students, including African Americans and Native Americans at about the same time (Holmes and Weiss 63–66). Since colleges began to allow women entrance during the Civil War in order to stay financially solvent, it is not unreasonable to interpret these changes in normal schools as consequences of upper-class women vacating the schools in favor of other opportunities.

Similarly, the case of Ellen Hyde, the principal of the Framingham Normal School from 1868 to 1898, is indicative of these tensions of gender and class in the preparation of teachers. Hyde incorporated current events, politics, literature, and sports into the curriculum at Framingham, let students there participate in their own self-government, and increased the connections with both southern free schools for former slaves and with schools on Native American reservations, eventually admitting students from both minority groups as prospective teachers. Hyde also advocated a high school diploma as a condition for admission, but was willing to keep students in the program until they mastered the material rather than allowing them to graduate after a particular period of time. For Hyde, teachers could be influential and the women who attended her normal school might go on to other careers besides teaching. At an 1886 graduation ceremony, she urged:

> Cultivate a broad interest in the world's welfare. It is among the possibilities of the future to make yourselves felt in the adjustment of capital and labor, in prison reform, in justice to the Indian and the Chinaman, in the true elevation of your own sex, in wiser social relations, in a more Christ-like christianity. Life that offers such opportunities is good and sweet; it may be grand. (Holmes and Weiss 68)

Advocating such possibilities for women, especially these women who were attending the normal school, was not, however, a view shared by others responsible for directing the school. One state-appointed school visitor, Kate Gannett Wells, who was publicly against the extension of suffrage to women, used her visits to tell the students that the education they were receiving would enable them to marry well, apparently because it would give them the cultural markers of the middle class. Hyde did not object to marriage, but understood her work to be that of preparing young women for careers, and she resisted efforts to include domestic studies in the curriculum. Such differences in outlook between Hyde and board members may have contributed to her decision to resign in the spring of 1898. It is probably no coincidence that immediately after her resignation, the board of directors abolished the advanced program and established a household arts program, the first in the United States (Holmes and Weiss 70–71).

Although I would not try to claim that all normal schools kept women from achieving professional status, or that all professional organizations limited the roles that women could play, these discursive exemplars demonstrate a consistent undercurrent of contradictions in the efforts to educate teachers in ways that would allow them to gain professional status or act as professionals. And, because most teachers did not receive specific preparation to teach before beginning to serve as classroom teachers, there were simultaneous efforts to provide some professional education to teachers who were already employed. However, even in these in-service programs, teachers were not afforded the professional standing that their years of experience or their employment status might suggest would have been appropriate.

Developing Teachers

Teacher institutes, sometimes called temporary normal schools, were a popular means of reeducating classroom teachers throughout the nineteenth century. Tracking the work of teacher institutes is complicated, however, because they overlapped with the efforts of normal schools and professional organizations. Elsbree credits Henry Barnard of Connecticut with starting the first teacher institute in 1839 as a precursor to normal schools in that state (155). And while institutes were apparently seen as a way of reaching teachers who were already employed in the schools, all were open to those who wanted to become teachers as well. One collection of documents from a summer teacher institute can be found at the University of North Carolina at Chapel Hill. Examining the materials from a southern state also allows me to stretch the contours of this project beyond New England and move to the latter part of the nineteenth century. Despite these differences in time and geography, the discourse patterns are remarkably similar to those I have already examined, and they include such features as faulting teachers while calling for their professionalization, suggesting specialized study but delivering review of subject matter, and contesting the meaning of teaching.

North Carolina Governor Vance's 1877 inaugural address, for example, proposed that the University of North Carolina at Chapel Hill begin a normal school and offer summer school sessions for public school teachers. The legislature authorized funds for white, male teachers to attend these institutes/normal schools and for a similar one to be started at the University at Fayetteville for black, male teachers. The universities, however, decided to invite women to participate if they paid their own expenses, and women did enroll in great numbers (Wilson 84). Vance's address includes many of the features seen in earlier pleas for teacher preparation in the northern states.

Taking a single paragraph point by point , Vance is

- linking the need for teachers to the need for better public schooling: "It is impossible to have an effective public school system without providing for the training of teachers."
- faulting current teachers' abilities: "The blind cannot lead the blind."
- defining teaching as more centered on the learner and

learning than on the transmission of knowledge: "Mere literary attainments are not sufficient to make its possessor a successful instructor. There must be added ability to influence the young and to communicate knowledge. There must be a mastery of the best modes of conducting schools, and of bringing out the latent possibilities, intellectual and moral, of the pupil's nature."
- proposing specific study related to teaching rather than general education in the subjects to be taught: "In some rare cases these qualities are inborn, but generally it is of vast advantage to teachers to be trained by those who have studied and mastered the methods, which have been found be [sic] experience to be the most successful in dispelling ignorance and inculcating knowledge."
- linking the need to prepare teachers to the numerical need for teachers: "There cannot possibly found [sic] in this State competent teachers for our public schools."
- reverting to a definition of teaching as relying on knowledge of basic subjects: "The records of the county examiners show that most of the applicants for the post of imparting knowledge to others are themselves deficient in the simplest elements of spelling, reading, arithmetic, and writing." (6–7)

Despite Vance's construction of teaching as requiring more than a review of content knowledge, the University of North Carolina normal school session of 1879 apparently covered only the usual common school subjects. At least the testing that resulted in teacher certification covered only the usual common school subjects. Complete records of curricula of the institute are unavailable, but a handwritten letter providing the scores for the teachers who were tested at the end of the summer session that year lists the areas examined as history, geography, reading, punctuation, writing and drawing, sounds, spelling, arithmetic, composition, grammar, algebra, and natural philosophy. Since only twenty-three of the forty-six applicants who took the test passed, it would appear that Vance's concern about the level of common learning was well founded and that North Carolina's early efforts to systematize teacher preparation faced the same difficulties of poorly prepared teachers that Cyrus Peirce had encountered earlier in the century in Massachusetts. In a slightly more public version of the tension Peirce expressed in his private diary entries, the letter accompanying the teachers' scores articulates the examining committee's deliberations.

> The committee were unanimous in the opinion that the standard of education in the state can be elevated only by thorough scholarship on the part of the teachers, and that a state certificate of scholarship and character ought to be given only to such teachers as, on examination, may be found to be fairly entitled to it. They believed, however, that the examination ought not to be so rigid as to exclude applicants altogether, and, therefore, they made a very lenient examination. (McIver)

If the committee believed that elevating the schools required "thorough scholarship" and that state certificates should only be issued to those entitled to claim both "scholarship and character," should we accept these subject areas as indicative of what this committee thought proved such abilities? Or, is the disclaimer that the committee made "a very lenient examination" an indication that these prospective teachers were examined on subjects considered easier than the advanced scholarship and expertise indicative of professional character? Either way, there is clearly a tension between the construction of the qualified teacher as one who has mastered basic knowledge and Governor Vance's rhetoric that "mere literary attainments are not sufficient to make its possessor a successful instructor."

The tension of these competing constructions of teaching cannot be dismissed as simply the difference between different writers, for the committee is careful to ask the university president to issue the "first grade certificates" with the scores in the various branches added to the certificate. Apparently, these examiners did not want their endorsement to be taken as a blanket of authority or expertise, but merely an indication that the recipient had passed a set of subject matter examinations. In fact, a close examination of the scores indicates that not only did half of those who took the exam fail completely, but some of the teachers passed with total scores of fifty (roughly 26 percent) on a scale where the best score would be thirteen and the worst possible would have been sixty-five. The best student in the group scored eighteen (72 percent), but the group average score was thirty-one (41 percent), hardly a sign of "thorough scholarship" or high standards, especially for a lenient exam.

Because the state had provided funds for men to attend the normal schools and the universities had extended the invitation to women who could afford to pay for themselves, we might expect that the women would have come from the upper class, would have had more access to earlier schooling, and would have therefore scored better on these examinations of basic knowledge. Only ten of the twenty-three who passed the test were women, however, and the document provides no indication of the gender of those who failed. The average score of the ten women who passed was 31.7, actually slightly worse than the average score for the men. Thus, at least on the slim evidence of this group of newly endorsed teachers, it does not appear that class or gender issues resulted in significant differences between male and female certification rates, at least in North Carolina. Since the summer institutes enrolled both prospective and already employed teachers, it is impossible to tell whether those who passed were teachers already holding positions in schools or were new recruits who may have just finished the primary grades themselves.

By 1885, the summer institutes for teachers in North Carolina had expanded to eight additional sites. But despite Peabody funds and legislative and public support, the University Normal School and its branch institutes were abolished in 1889 and replaced with separate institutes in the ninety-two different counties (Wilson 85). The University of North Carolina's Department of Pedagogy did not reemerge until 1913 under the new title of School of Education

(Wilson 86), but a 1923 University of North Carolina record includes a historical note stating that the summer school teacher institute sessions were revived from 1894–1904 and again in 1907. This evidence indicates the uneven efforts at preparing beginning teachers and offering further training to teachers already employed.

The announcement for the 1881 summer session at Chapel Hill provides another example of an appeal to different kinds of teachers. The circular announcing the sessions begins with language that sounds like professional training instead of only content review:

> Teaching is not only a science, but an art. The Normal School will therefore be, as heretofore, under the charge of trained experts, who for years have made methods a study, and have had large practical experience in their working. (University Normal School)

The circular proceeds, however, to list a "scheme of instruction" that clearly involves all who attend in a study of the branches of the common school as well as exposure to professional topics:

I. Regular Instruction for all Students, including
   (1) Daily Recitations and Lectures on Arithmetic (mental and written), English Grammar and Analysis, Orthography, Reading, Phonetics, and Geography;
   (2) Daily Lectures before the whole School, on School Organization and Discipline, Methods of Instruction, the relation of Teacher, Parent and Child, &c.;
   (3) Daily Drill in Vocal Music.
II. Special Instruction for Advanced Students, in the following branches: Chemistry, including Laboratory Practice, Latin (two classes), Algebra, Book-Keeping and Penmanship.
III. Classes will be formed of pupils to be taught by the

more advanced Normal Students, under the supervision of the Professors. In this connection will be exhibited the system and Methods of Graded Schools.
IV. A series of Lectures on the Geology of North Carolina, by Professor Kerr, the State Geologist.
V. Lectures by distinguished educators and specialists of North Carolina and other States. (University Normal School)

The program for the County Institute in Massachusetts a year later (1882) reproduced by Elsbree is actually much narrower in its focus, including lectures in arithmetic analysis, drawing, botany, geography, language and grammar, mineralogy, reading along with the more professionally oriented topics of methods of assigning lessons and hearing recitations, lessons in teaching color, and school government and moral instruction (360).

Neither of these documents for teacher institutes shows any distinction between the teacher who is already employed and the student who wished to enter teaching. "Advanced Students" in the North Carolina circular does not indicate a student who is advanced because of experience in the classroom, but rather a teacher who wishes to work with students at a higher grade level. The lack of distinction suggests that those who prepared these courses of study saw the already employed as having very little professional expertise or standing, and reports of attendance do not bother to separate the kinds of teachers who attended these institutes.

The point in reviewing these documents is not to suggest that the South was more or less advanced in its pedagogical preparation of teachers than the North, or that these early institutes were somehow ineffective. Rather, the evidence demonstrates that even when the discursive representations of teacher preparation emphasizes specialized expertise, the practice of preparing teachers has consistently been to balance providing content knowledge with offering more specific study in teaching that knowledge to others. The assumption that simply having information would enable someone to teach has coexisted with a concern for the effectiveness of teaching.

And, while preparation for effectiveness has most often been practiced as the "natural" nurturing role of the "mother," it has been presented in discursive constructions as dependent on the expertise derived from studies of pedagogy, including consideration of the learner's development, theories of knowledge, and methods of instruction. Because the expansion of schooling required more and more teachers, the study of pedagogical topics was often sacrificed, certification was based on competency in subject matter, and measures of effectiveness were limited to the "natural" ethic of care. Moreover, even when teachers gained employment that would suggest they had met at least a local hiring committee's standards for professional work, others within the profession did not treat them as experts or professionals. At least in teacher institutes, classroom teachers were lumped with novices no matter how much experience or prior training they may have had.

Thus, beginning as soon as thirty years after the first appearance in the United States of a call for a special school to prepare teachers, concerns about education had shifted to using a language that blamed teachers for the faults of schools. Although the public discourse called for professionalizing teachers, the language and arguments employed in these discussions simultaneously undercut the possibility that teaching would be accepted as a profession equal to other professions because it precluded teachers from the public discussions of education by omitting any expectation that they be prepared for public speaking or debate. Furthermore, these reform efforts used external rather than internal evaluators of teachers' abilities, violating another central condition of professional status. Likewise, rather than redefining teaching as requiring specialized knowledge and thus shifting teachers into the realm of professionals, those who argued for the creation of teacher preparation programs began by articulating lesser levels of subject matter knowledge and only gradually began to include specialized study centered on the learner. Even when specialized knowledge was included in the plans for teacher preparation, the programs themselves did not consistently provide the specialized, intellectual preparation necessary for teachers to claim the expertise of professionals. In fact, admitting students with less prior schooling, those who were seen as already less worthy by virtue of their economic or class status, and claiming teaching as connected to the natural traits of mothering served to gender teaching as feminine, leaving those aspects of education that were outside the classroom as the more powerful, more intellectual domain of the masculine.

These discursive patterns continued throughout the nineteenth century, repeating themselves in the southern states later in the century as schooling expanded in that region much later than in New England and the Northwest Territories. In the next chapter, I show how the patterns persist as higher education emerges at the end of the twentieth century to be the newest level of "common schooling" for American students.

3 / Reshaping Professional Training

In leaping from the beginning of the twentieth century to its end, from the teaching of elementary teachers to the difficulties within higher education, I do not mean to suggest that these time periods or contexts are easily congruent or that the intervening years are inconsequential. It is possible, however, to hear the echoes of earlier arguments in current discussions, to recognize the conceptions of the past embedded in the language we inherit. The focus here is on this discourse, and this project assumes that it ought to be possible to use what we learn from the study of our inherited discourse to better understand the uses, and misuses, of language, and to forge new conceptions by closer attention to the constructions implied in rhetoric. My claim at the beginning of chapter 2 was this: although the attempts to improve education by improving teachers has employed a rhetoric of professionalization, these efforts have not provided the kind of education that would enable teachers to make independent judgments that would qualify them as professionals. The Boyer report, which moves this call for professionalizing teaching to the newest level of common education, the university, repeats a pattern of rhetorical constructions that suggests its efforts, too, will fail to alter the cultural structures that devalue teaching and teachers.

The first chapter suggests that higher education, and the literacy level it represents, has become the newest level of "common schooling." Indeed, the public criticism directed at higher education for the last two decades is a sign of this new level of literacy expectations and expanding educational opportunities. As would be expected from the pattern established in the historic documents examined in chapter 2, the public criticism of higher education has mutated into a concern about the quality of teaching and teachers at this higher level and efforts have proliferated to improve both the existing university teachers and the preparation given to those who wish to become university teachers.

It is not the case that faculty development programs or training for graduate students did not exist before the most recent public critique of higher education. Indeed, Betty Pytlik's review of the history of graduate student preparation provides examples of professional concern about the preparation of college teachers of composition as early as 1900. Nevertheless, it is clear that the amount of public and professional attention to these issues has increased dramatically in the last few years, and the Boyer report is an interesting exemplar of the discourse of these efforts. An examination of this single example of the response to public criticism of higher education illustrates the ways the historical patterns are repeated at this new level of common school expansion and the recurrence of contradictory definitions of teaching and the reeducation of teachers as professionals.

Background

"Reinventing Undergraduate Education: A Blueprint for America's Research Universities" is the document produced by the Boyer Commission on Educating Undergraduates in the Research University that has come to be known simply as "the Boyer report." The eleven-member commission began its work under the auspices of the Carnegie Foundation for the Advancement of Teaching in mid-1995. During the second meeting of the commission in December 1995, Ernest Boyer, who had been the director of the Carnegie Foundation, died, and the subsequent adjustments within the foundation made the commission decide to publish its report as an independent document rather than as a report from the foundation (Boyer Commission).

Like other foundation-sponsored projects, the commission comprised selected, well-known members of the academic community who agreed to work on the project. Members were chosen primarily through the informal networks of Boyer and Shirley Strum Kenny, president of the State University of New York at Stony Brook

(Kenny). It was Kenny who originally conceived of the project as a way of making concrete recommendations to improve undergraduate instruction in the face of public criticism of higher education, particularly criticism directed at research universities. As a member of the Carnegie Foundation's board of directors, Kenny had known Boyer and had admired his work to improve education for years before suggesting that he form a commission to document and argue for research universities' unique role in educating undergraduates.

Like other commissions, the Boyer group met irregularly and drew primarily on the expertise of its members, who had been chosen to represent a range of disciplines, institutions, and geographic locations. The commission also located and heard testimony from other experts, particularly those who headed research universities at which innovation in undergraduate instruction was already underway. Unlike other Carnegie documents, however, the final report of the Boyer group was thoughtfully crafted as a public document, printed with marginal graphics to illustrate specific facts, examples from various institutions, and cartoonlike illustrations of key points. The report was also made available on a Web site established at Kenny's home institution, State University of New York at Stony Brook, and announced on a number of academic electronic message boards as well as in the media. The Web version initially stripped the document of the marginal graphics, thereby eliminating much of the supporting factual evidence for the commission's conclusions, but the widespread dissemination of its recommendations have lent the authority of published "blue-ribbon" expertise and foundation clout to a large number of institutional and departmental initiatives. In fact, the close connections between the Carnegie Foundation initiatives to improve higher education and to support the scholarship of teaching and learning and the Pew Foundation projects related to the preparation of future professors are apparent in both the final report and the SUNY–Stony Brook Web site links to institutional initiatives.

Tracing the interconnections of foundation support for such reform efforts in education is beyond the scope of this project, as is the history of foundation involvement in educational reform and higher education. That such tracing and history would complicate the reading of these documents seems to me obvious, and readers should be alert to the not-quite-invisible hand of these nonacademic, nonuniversity, nongovernmental professional educators behind the document. I do not mean to suggest that these offstage actors are somehow illegitimate or that their motives are necessarily suspect; indeed, there are many people connected to these foundations who, like Kenny, simultaneously occupy roles within universities, and much of the work of these foundations is exemplary. I mean to suggest only that there is much about such foundations and their workings that is not generally known and is thus usually ignored as a force in the scholarship about schooling, higher education, or particular disciplines and universities.

But even if the Boyer report had not made an impact in public and academic circles when it first appeared, and even if it does not turn out to be a document of lasting historical importance, it is, nonetheless, an important exemplar of the rhetoric of reforming higher education that responded to the public criticism about undergraduate instruction and the poor quality of teaching in the nation's premier universities that arose in the 1980s and continued through the end of the century.

The full, forty-four-page report includes a preface, an overview, a brief discussion of the uniqueness and importance of research universities, and an "Academic Bill of Rights" for undergraduates in research universities before it gets to the heart of the document: the ten suggestions for changing undergraduate education. Each of the ten suggestions is organized with a brief statement explaining the titled suggestion, a justification presented as a set of assertions with minimal supporting evidence, subsections that describe specific components of the suggestions, and a summary list of four to eight specific recommendations. Thus, each of the ten suggestions has additional recommendations built in, which offers readers a broad set of specific and general ideas and preserves the simplicity of a list of ten key suggestions.

Many of the ten suggestions cover familiar terrain for those involved in introductory courses in composition:

1. make research-based learning the standard;
2. construct an inquiry-based freshman year;
3. build on the freshman foundation;
4. remove barriers to interdisciplinary education;
5. link communication skills and course work;
6. use information technology creatively;
7. culminate with a capstone experience;
8. educate graduate students as apprentice teachers;
9. change faculty-reward systems; and
10. cultivate a sense of community.

Within these pages, though, are also many of the patterns of discourse I outlined in previous chapters.

Faulting Teachers Again

Like earlier documents, the Boyer report claims both the importance of education to the American public and its faults as reasons for the suggestions that follow. The overview, for example, reads as follows:

> In a great many ways the higher education system of the United States is the most remarkable in the world. Half of the high school graduates in the United States now gain some experience in college and universities; we are, as a country, attempting to create an educated population on a scale never known before. In the higher education system in the United States, the research universities have played a leading role: the country's 125 research universities make up only 3 per cent of the total number of institutions of higher learning, yet they confer 32 per cent of the baccalaureate degrees, and 56 per cent of the baccalaureates earned by recent recipients of science and engineering doctorates (1991–95). Nevertheless, the research universities have too often failed, and continue to fail, their undergraduate populations. Again and again, universities are

guilty of an advertising practice they would condemn in the commercial world. Some of their instructors are likely to be badly trained or even untrained teaching assistants who are groping their way toward a teaching technique; some others may be tenured drones who deliver set lectures from yellowed notes, making no effort to engage the bored minds of the students in front of them. (Boyer Commission 5–6)

Like the rhetorical frames used in the early 1800s by the educational reformers James Carter, Walter Johnson, and Samuel Hall that we examined in the preceding chapter, the desire for better and more education that begins the Boyer report's overview mutates quickly into faulting teachers. And, although the margins of the overview section include charts showing the percentage of the population in various countries that receives university education, the kinds of institutions at which science and engineering students get their degrees, the growth in degrees since 1969, and the kinds and percentage of different students at different institutions, no evidence is provided to support the claims that teaching is substandard at research institutions. As I have shown, the problem of bad teaching has been such a commonplace since the early nineteenth century that it can be treated as so obvious to all readers that it needs no support.

I do not mean to suggest that the Boyer Commission has made false claims; anyone closely associated with higher education knows that some undergraduates may indeed have teachers who are "badly trained," "tenured drones," or "groping their way toward a teaching technique." Rather, the point is that the commission is not simply reporting the conditions of higher education in a neutral or objective way. The discourse of faulting teachers and linking those faults to desires to improve and expand education is a long-standing cultural practice, a rhetorical trope. Like other rhetorical tropes, this one can be employed precisely because it is so familiar and "natural" that it does not need substantiation. Once employed, tropes set up expectations for other familiar moves that take over the structure of the discourse. Just as the emplotment of history as a narrative demands a narrative closure (see, e.g., White *Content*), using the trope of faulting teachers requires a proposal to correct these faults, and the Boyer report complies.

The higher prestige associated simply with college education in earlier years is, in the Boyer report, linked specifically to research institutions. Given the focus on research universities, the claim that these institutions are superior is, perhaps, to be expected. Sprinkled throughout the introductory pages, however, are the reasons these institutions can be considered superior to other forms of higher education. In case readers do not already know, the Boyer report takes pains to remind readers that research universities are classified by the Carnegie Foundation on the basis of the larger amount of money they receive for research and the larger number of advanced degrees they award, and, it reminds as well, Nobel laureates are most often professors at research universities. Both the Carnegie Foundation rankings and the Nobel Prizes employ the criteria of groups outside the control of the profession of educators, which my readers will recognize as another long-standing feature of American education.

The report goes on to explain that research universities have a broader outlook that attracts more international students and are able to supplement the expenses for promising lower-class students, thus attracting a wider range of students—features that appeal to the open-mindedness and meritocracy associated with American values. Furthermore, the report declares, some states require students to attend lesser colleges first and move to the research universities only for their final two years of study—the study that would be the most advanced and specialized—a suggestion that student ability (and age) dictates the structure of higher education rather than the material costs of instruction versus research. In each of these features, the metaphors of bigger, more, and better are also already a "natural" part of the language of description.

Again, my point is not that research universities do not have the features the Boyer report describes; rather, I wish to point out the way that commonplace language can obscure the assumptions and values that are already a part of the landscape of our discussions and efforts at reform. Might it not be possible, for example, to argue that an institution that graduates only a few students or that concentrates its resources in only a few areas must put more careful attention into its work than a university that tries to do too much for too many? Is this not exactly the argument made by those who value the small liberal arts college over the research university? Could we not argue, as many people at open-admission state institutions do, that a university that can educate the range of beginning students who come through its doors is "better" than a university that eliminates students who need special attention and concentrates only on the already bright and motivated? In other words, are the values assigned to research universities not already privileged precisely because they are the values assigned to research universities? Indeed, the Carnegie classification of institutions on the basis of the degrees they award and the amount of research money they have has been recognized as so slanted against the values of good teaching, so misused to confer status, that the foundation itself is in the process of proposing an alternative means of ranking institutions (McCormick).

Embedded in the report as well is the shift to pay better attention to the learner. Research institutions, defined by their attention to knowledge making, new discoveries, and original creations, are being urged by the commission to care for their undergraduate students. The inclusion of the "Academic Bill of Rights" and even the ten suggestions themselves reposition the university professor as responsible for student learning, not merely for the creation of new knowledge. Like the documents addressed to an earlier level of common schooling, the Boyer report thus contests the meaning of teaching as it has existed at research institutions, adding a level of client care and service to the expectations for those who make academics their profession. Careful to distance their goals from those of liberal arts colleges, though, the Boyer report uses language that is linked to knowledge making rather than student development. Notice, for example, that each of the ten suggestions is given in an imperative form so that the nouns are usually a form of knowing rather than people. Only in the eighth suggestion, the one I examine more closely in a moment, do any of the people of the institution appear. It is the freshman *year* rather than freshmen who appear in the second suggestion; it is the faculty reward *systems* rather than faculty who are the focus of suggestion nine.

In effect, then, the style of the report replicates the kinds of rhetorical moves seen in earlier examples—a style that obscures the inherent contradictions even as it appears to reason carefully and persuasively. And, like earlier documents, the substance of the report continues to create deep contradictions as it argues for increasing the value and status of teaching, but denying the kind of education that would actually produce meaningful changes in our cultural conceptions of teaching. These contradictions are most clearly seen in the section on preparing graduate students to teach, which I turn to next.

Teaching Graduate Students to Be Teachers

The eighth suggestion is the one most relevant to this project because it focuses on teaching teachers. The second longest of the ten suggestions, "educate graduate students as apprentice teachers" is the only one to include both "signs of change" case studies and "the facts" as marginal material of illustration or support. The suggestion begins: "Although graduate education is not at the center of our concern, clearly the metamorphosis of undergraduate education at research universities can not occur without suitable adjustments in the way that graduate students are prepared for their professional roles" (Boyer Commission 28).

In this slight variation on the historical trope that education can be improved by improving teachers, the report asserts that the connection between graduate preparation and reforming undergraduate studies is "clear." The assumption here, of course, is that readers already know the significant role graduate students play in teaching undergraduates at research universities. Interestingly, the logic of turning to graduate student preparation is not supported by facts about the number of undergraduates taught by graduate students or by the absence of research faculty from undergraduate classrooms. Instead, the section is corroborated with figures about the number of graduate students who will go on to teaching, though not usually at research institutions; since more than half of all doctoral students will go into academic jobs, the commission argues, and few of those will be at research universities, graduate education should not neglect its role of preparing college teachers. The statistics provided both within the text and the marginal graphs confirm the large percentage of doctoral students who plan to go into teaching, the numbers and percentage of doctorates who find employment with two-year, four-year, and research institutions, and the employment distribution of doctorates since 1975 across academe, industry, and government sectors. Although the report presents these statistics as if doctorates going into teaching positions were something of a new phenomenon, they are actually long-standing features of the degree. In fact, a speaker at the 1912 Modern Language Association conference noted that "the Ph.D. as at present conceived is not a teacher's degree but an investigator's degree; most graduates must teach, for there is little opportunity of making a livelihood by investigation" (Cox 207).

The other half of the report's assertion—that graduate education has been neglecting its role of preparing college teachers—is treated as instinctively correct; no facts or figures are offered in support of this claim. Instead, a subsection entitled "reshaping professional training" presents a narrative version of the common experience that includes

- students going directly from undergraduate studies into graduate school with no time to adjust to new demands or increased expectations;
- new graduate students being asked to teach undergraduate courses outside their own field of interest [composition being taught by literature majors is included as a specific example of such a teaching assignment];

- graduate students entering the classroom with little or no training; and,
- no "serious training in pedagogy" offered to new teachers resulting in stress for the instructors and poor instruction for undergraduates. (29)

The end of this section repeats the assertion that there is a disjunction between the training graduate students receive and the careers they will enter. The assertion is developed once again with a mininarrative of the common expectations of employers (for clear communication, teamwork, expertise, problem solving, and critical thinking) and the common training offered in graduate programs as "intensive work in narrowly defined subjects and meticulous training in the technical skills required for research projects; it is the unstated assumption that the other expectations will be met without organized effort" (30).

"Reshaping Professional Training" thus seems an odd title for the section since the explication offered is not really an example of "reshaping," but rather a listing of conditions that prompts the call for reshaping. The juxtaposition of *professional* and *training* would also seem, at first, a kind of internal contradiction since training would usually appear in connection with more simplistic jobs that require little intellectual engagement, and professional is, as we have seen, a term that is associated less with the economics of securing a job than with the identity and authority of the upper-class careers. Thus, to speak of graduate doctoral programs as having a responsibility to provide "professional education" would have been, perhaps, more appropriate than to speak of profession making as if it were a job-training program. But, of course, all the data and narratives offered in this section are about the forces involved in getting and keeping a job after graduation from such programs, and, in this sense, the writers are correct to identify their interest in the issue as one of training. Because the jobs these graduates will secure are likely to be lifelong career choices in the profession of education, the report implicitly reasons, graduate programs are indeed preparing professionals, though they are not necessarily doing so with much conscious attention to what becoming a professional might require. The conception of teaching embedded in this use of the term *professional* in this suggestion is one of a life's work, a full-time job. Teaching here has become simply "work," a point I return to in the next chapter.

Two additional subsections follow "Reshaping Professional Training." In the first, "Restoring Communication," the importance of all graduate students knowing how to communicate both orally and in writing is asserted. In the second, "Solving the Teaching Crisis," the claim that "the reconstitution of doctoral programs will have a profound effect on undergraduate education" is followed by a brief discussion of how teaching undergraduates to communicate well and to participate in inquiry will produce better-prepared graduate students. Although these statements are presented as if their truth were undeniable, their very presence repeats the historical pattern of faulting the ability of current, teaching graduate students; current graduate students must not communicate well or there would be no reason to "restore" communicative competence. What is not spoken, but many readers surely recognized, is the gesture toward the public criticism of research institutions for employing foreign-born graduate students with less-than-fluent English proficiency to teach undergraduates at these expensive and elite research institutions. The logic of the second statement—that improving graduate education will also improve undergraduate education—is actually a version of the long-standing link between the "character" of the teacher and the character of the schools; improve the teacher and the schools will yield better students.

Similarly, "teaching is a difficult enough task in any setting, and in a research university the difficulties are magnified" is offered as unquestionable, though many readers might wish for at least an example of how research universities magnify the difficulties of teaching. Still, the trope at work is the need to create problems that can only be fixed with the proposal to provide "professionals," in this case graduate students prepared specifically to teach in research universities.

The seven specific recommendations that follow this discursive discussion of the suggestion that graduate programs prepare teachers parallel many of the faults the report has listed earlier and include

1. allowing graduate students time to adjust to graduate school before entering the classroom [which matches the fault of not giving graduate students time to adjust];
2. offering seminars, supervision, mentoring and regular discussion to support graduate students learning to teach [which parallels the fault of asking graduate students to teach with little or no training];
3. teaching graduate students to promote learning by inquiry rather than the old models of transferring knowledge [which supports the primary goal of the entire report];
4. emphasizing writing and speaking in graduate courses [which counters the fault that graduate students are not competent themselves];
5. encouraging graduate students to use technology in creative ways [which matches another of the report's primary interests in promoting technology and creative methods of instruction];
6. fairly compensating graduate students for the time they spend teaching [which addresses the common concern for material conditions that will be the focus of my next chapter]; and,
7. encouraging graduate students to value teaching by offering special rewards for outstanding teaching and financial awards to outstanding teaching assistants [which partially counters the fault of asking graduate students to teach outside their areas of interest by hoping to make teaching an interest, or at least financially valuable, for all graduate students]. (29, 31)

While it is easy to agree with these recommendations, to see them as possible to implement, and to recognize the way they reinforce the other suggestions the commission is making or the faults they have identified, it is difficult to understand how any or all of these suggestions constitute "reshaping professional training," a solution to the "teaching crisis," or viable ways to "educate graduate students as apprentice teachers." In fact, many if not all, of these recommendations are already in place in universities across the country and have had little impact on the value attributed to teaching or the overall shape of graduate programs. It is quite possible to implement any one, or even several, of these recommendations without changing anything about the overall structure of graduate education or the value that is attributed to teaching.

Take, for example, the recommendation that graduate apprentice teachers be assisted through seminars in teaching. Such "teaching seminars" are a routine practice in English departments that have graduate students teaching first-year composition, but the commission's proposal does not say anything about the content of the seminar. As we saw in the historical documents focused on common school teacher preparation and teacher institutes, what teachers are taught in their preparation courses can vary a great deal, from basic content knowledge to theories of child development, cognition, or classroom management. Since the commission has already named literature students being used to teach first-year composition as an example of one of the problems of graduate student education, they must have known that the content of these seminars matches the local conditions of specific institutional settings, conditions like whether the program funds master's level students or only those pursuing the doctorate, or whether the department offers a degree in composition studies or only degrees in literature and literary criticism. Staying silent on the difference between content knowledge and pedagogical preparation does little to ensure the kinds of preparation that would actually alter undergraduate teaching. Turning to the specifics of such seminars in English departments, and their history, will further illustrate the significance of the commission's failure to address this issue.

Teaching Seminars and the Contestation of Teaching

Seminars specifically designed to prepare graduate students to teach, especially to teach composition, have apparently existed since at least the early 1900s. In 1912, for example, Chester Noyes Greenough of Harvard University reported to the College Section of the National Council of Teachers of English (NCTE) on his "experiment" in teaching such a course. The official course description was given as:

> English 67—English Composition. Practice in Writing, in the Criticism of Manuscript, and in the Instruction by Conferences and Lectures. Discussion of the Principles of Composition and of the Organization and Management of Courses in English Composition. (109)

The description of this experiment, however, reveals many of the same difficulties that faced the teachers in early normal schools since Greenough first complains of the writing ability of these graduate students and admits to spending more than half of the time teaching these would-be teachers "to write well themselves" (111). What pedagogical training there is in this course is described as observation of student writing, practice in responding to writing, and practice in conferencing and class activities. Nothing is said about the reading these students do, the theories of writing or learning they might be asked to consider, or the ways they might be encouraged to develop a conception of their own role as teachers. Indeed, Fred Newton Scott criticizes Greenough's course later in the year as "mainly another course, added to those already offered, in the art and practice of writing English. This looks, no doubt, in the right direction, but, after all, goes only a little way. Good writers, to be candid, are not always good teachers" (Scott 457). Such a course, then, though meant to be a kind of professional education, once again did not provide the expertise or foundational knowledge that would equip these early college-level teachers to claim a professional status as teachers. Instead, it was designed to function as does job training: prepare the would-be teacher with enough basic skill to ensure some level of consistency in courses designed—in Beecher's words—by "one directing mind."

Offering any courses to prepare college teachers was not, however, the norm at this time, so Greenough is justified in considering his efforts "an experiment." The Modern Language Association's Committee on the Preparation of College Teachers of English, formed in late 1912, conducted a survey of heads of English departments at large universities, teachers of undergraduates holding doctorates and university presidents. This work was continued by a committee constituted by the NCTE, which reported the results in the January 1916 edition of the *English Journal*, which, as the only journal of the organization at that time, addressed all levels and kinds of English teaching. Among the findings of these committees were

- only 12 of 28 department heads responding to the initial Modern Language Association (MLA) survey thought it necessary to offer any distinct effort to prepare graduate students and only 4 were then offering any such course; 9 of those rejecting the need for special training to teach thought that "a good man will learn how to teach by teaching";
- in the NCTE's subsequent survey of more colleges, 26 out of 57 responding department chairs reported offering no courses in the preparation for teaching, 2 offered courses specifically for college-level teaching, and 17 offered a course on teaching English without distinguishing the level; the rest offered supervision, apprenticeships or other forms of preparation not related to course work;
- 21% of the 71 teachers of undergraduates holding Ph.D.s in the initial MLA survey were critical of their graduate studies as a preparation for teaching, but only 13 suggested adding a course in teaching as a possible improvement;
- of the 278 undergraduate teachers (not limited to those with Ph.D.s) surveyed in the subsequent study, only 24 reported having specific professional training to teach and only 17 listed it as having proved the "most valuable" to their subsequent teaching assignments. (Committee on the Preparation of College Teachers of English, "Report" 20–29)

When the committee made its final recommendations reported in the 1918 *English Journal,* it suggested that departments offer two courses specifically in the preparation to teach college English, and that the courses include

a) A consideration of the aims of regular college work in the subject.
b) A survey of college courses in English now in operation or projected.
c) A critical outline of material and method in the teaching of composition (or literature) to Freshmen and Sophomores.
d) Observation of teaching and, if possible, participation in the actual work of the college classroom.
e) Critical evaluation of actual material of the classroom, such as students' themes, textbooks, outlines, etc.
f) A study of the problem of testing and grading.
g) Familiarity with the literature of the subject.
h) Familiarity with the work of secondary schools, their conditions and limitations, and the necessary relations of such work to the courses in the junior college. (Committee on the Preparation of College Teachers of English, "Tentative" 63)

Notice that this list includes items that are related to the immediate practical work of composition teaching (evaluation of classroom materials and consideration of aims of the course), items that can apply to teaching in general (the problem of testing and grading), and items that focus on the institutionalized structure of American education (the work of secondary schools). There is no indication that this committee saw teaching as an intellectual activity requiring the kinds of theoretical foundation, research strategies, or specialized expertise of other disciplines except perhaps in the ambiguous phrases like "critical evaluation," "critical outline," or "study." Interestingly, though, this early list does not indicate much attention to the learner or to mental development that emerged in the documents from earlier in the century addressed to the common school teachers. I take the absence of this attention to the learner as an indication that, in 1912, concern about college-level teaching was still focused on the much earlier conception of teaching as knowledge transference. Likewise, while these recommendations are much more thorough than any program found in the committee's earlier surveys, and are, in fact, more thorough than what is known to have existed in much of the subsequent century, the special attention to teaching necessary for graduate students in English was significantly undercut by the committee's own concluding recommendation, which reads: "Professional preparation of the kind outlined above should be honored with a special degree indicating that the holder is interested primarily in teaching rather than in advanced and highly specialized research" (63). Thus, the value of intellectual study and the expertise associated with professionals and with the "specialized research" of modern American universities was segregated from knowledge of, study in, or practices of teaching. And, this vacating of intellectual activity from the meaning of teaching is an indication that the term and the work had become so thoroughly feminized that it no longer mattered whether the actual individuals doing the teaching were male or female or whether they worked with children or young adults.

The contradiction of a committee constituted to make recommendations for all college English teachers separating teaching from research is all the more apparent in a note from the editor in a later issue the same year commenting on the criticism directed at college teachers then appearing in popular and professional journals. The editor, James Fleming Hosic of the Chicago Normal School, also chaired the NCTE committee. He wrote: "The causes of ineffective teaching are to be traced to the policy of the administrators, who have not regarded good teaching as the most important aspect of a professor's activities. Emphasis has been placed upon success in research. To get good teaching we must reward it" (Hosic 144). Of course, universities did not alter the reward structure to value teaching more than research, but the committee's recommendations led to the creation of the doctor of arts degree, a terminal degree focused on teaching that never obtained the status of the doctor of philosophy and was eliminated from most departments by the end of the century. I can but imagine, then, the way Hosic compromised his own views in order to arrive at a report his committee could endorse.

Similarly, a half century later in the early editions of the journal for the newly created Conference on College Composition and Communication (CCCC), there is evidence that some members of the profession were still concerned about the preparation graduate students received in teaching. There is also evidence that what such a preparation should involve was still far from standardized. Harold Allen of the University of Minnesota reported on his research of forty-seven institutions in the May 1952 issue of the organization's journal *College Composition and Communication (CCC)*, for example, noting, "What is being done to prepare college teachers of English is just as inadequate and outmoded as the old Model T would be on a modern express highway" (3). Allen records his interviews with English department chairs as largely repeating the same assumptions the 1912 MLA survey found: that teaching did not require specialized training and so anyone with a doctorate was qualified to teach. That Hosic committee recommendations had not been widely implemented for the majority of English doctoral students should come as no surprise since the report itself made attention to teaching a lesser degree, unequal to the research and scholarly interests of doctoral programs.

Furthermore, Allen reports, the few courses on teaching that were offered were not taught regularly; even at the University of Michigan, for example—which "has a fairly long record with such a course," dating at least to 1925, when Allen himself took it under the direction of Charles C. Fries—a pedagogical course had not been offered for three years. And, when it was offered, it consisted of a series of lectures by senior members of the department on "good teaching" (5). Of the six other colleges Allen found that offered (or had offered) courses aimed at college-level teaching, most were enrolling students interested in high school or junior college positions but not the doctoral students who actually hoped to teach at colleges or universities (5–6).

Irregular, ad hoc staff meetings sufficed as teacher preparation at most universities, Allen found, but the content and structure of these meetings varied greatly. Some centered primarily on administrative issues such as scheduling and were held as rarely as twice a year. Most schools, however, held one or more meetings focused on standardizing grading practices by having teachers compare the grades they gave on sample student papers. Harvard, however, had developed regular meetings that required teachers to discuss "broad educational issues as well as the minutiae of the course itself," and the University of Illinois's practice of bringing in guest speakers like the editor of *CCC* had led to an increase in membership in CCCC from that program.

Current descriptions of teaching seminars, even in English departments where they have an established role, are not easily available since they are often not given the same standing as other graduate courses, because there is so much variety in what is included on department Web sites and because different institutions have very different traditions surrounding how they represent course aims and objections. When such descriptions are available, the tensions between epistemologies are, however, still more than apparent. The descriptions offered of three different, institutionally required teaching seminars serves to illustrate my concerns.

At the University of Michigan English Department "Pedagogical Training for Ph.D. Students" provides an overview directed to the prospective graduate student:

> The English Department gives continuing attention to the pedagogical training of Graduate Student Instructors (GSIs); this training includes courses on pedagogy and an extensive system of mentoring.... Generally students begin teaching in their second year, usually by leading discussion sections attached to large undergraduate lecture courses. A required pedagogy course, taught by one member of the faculty, accompanies this initial teaching assignment; the course provides guidance in professional preparation for teaching undergraduate courses. The training includes faculty

visits to the GSI's section, help with designing courses and writing course descriptions and syllabuses, strategies for leading discussion sections, methods of grading and the like. (University of Michigan Department of English)

This description of the pedagogical preparation suggests a carefully constructed and systematic progression from assisting in a course to teaching a course independently. It is also clear that graduate students are given time to adjust to graduate study before assuming classroom duties, just as the Boyer report recommends. The University of Michigan's description further supports the Boyer report in recognizing the need to be prepared to teach by taking a course, though since this course is delayed until the graduate student is already engaged in teaching, it is apparent that at Michigan the course functions more as an institutionalized support system than as preparation for classroom assignment.

Notice that Michigan's course includes specific teaching strategies ("leading discussion sections, methods of grading and the like"), though there is no indication that such strategies are positioned within a study of student learning, curriculum design, or a principled understanding of education in general or English instruction in particular. Despite the phrase suggesting that multiple courses in pedagogy are available and required ("this training includes courses on pedagogy"), a review of the course descriptions for 2000 through fall 2002 reveals only one course that could be clearly identified as required and connected to teaching, a three credit course entitled "Pedagogy." Unlike other course descriptions for the department, however, the description for "Pedagogy" lists no texts, gives no indication of the evaluation procedures, and, for at least two years, had two faculty members assigned to it, probably because, as I show subsequently, these faculty members also made observation visits to classes taught by each of the graduate students enrolled in the seminar. The fall 2000 and 2001 descriptions are identical though they are taught by different pairs of faculty members, another sign that the course functions differently from typical graduate seminars. That description for the course reads:

> This two-semester course is designed to give you guidance, advice and support as you begin your teaching career. During the first semester, we will address issues relevant to the job of teaching assistant: how to organize discussions, how to negotiate your own and your students' relations with the lectures and the professor, grading, strategies for managing office hours and individual consultations, and so on. The second semester will be devoted to ongoing support, and to helping you prepare to teach your own course in the fall: how to pick a theme, design a syllabus, pace assignments, manage assessments, and so on. One of the primary aims of the course is to provide you with a space to discuss anxieties and achievements, but we will also follow a structured program designed to focus on specific aspects of work in the classroom. In addition, we will make regular visits to your classrooms so that we can give you specific feedback on your own strengths and weaknesses. We won't be able to take all the stress out of teaching, but we will emphasize its pleasures as well as its pains. The course will meet regularly for the first four weeks of the fall semester and then every other week thereafter. In the winter semester, we will meet five times. You enroll in the course for 3 credits only during the fall term. This course is required of all 2nd year Language & Literature and English & Women's Studies students. (Henderson and Whittier-Ferguson)

Particularly striking in this course description is the unusual structure for a graduate seminar (structuring the class sessions over two terms, but awarding the credit in only one term, for example), and its unusual goal of reducing stress and "emphasizing pleasures and pains" of teaching. Issues are "addressed," but there is no indication that students must read or produce anything in relation to those issues; no papers are required, no assignments are listed, and though preparing "to teach your own course" is a part of the work of this seminar, there is no clear indication that students must have an independent course ready by the end of the year. What materials would represent this readiness to teach an independent course are left unmentioned and invisible. And, since these students are taking the seminar during their initial teaching assignment, they clearly must have some teaching materials for a course already in hand.

Like "teaching seminars," described in historical documents or easily found at other institutions, the University of Michigan course is more like a "practicum," "workshop," or "lab" than like other graduate seminars offered by the department, though it would certainly meet the commission's suggestion of "offering seminars, mentoring and regular discussion to support graduate students learning to teach." Nothing in this course description, however, suggests that prospective teachers are learning to consider, or develop in students, any of the values that the commission establishes as the basis of learning: inquiry, interdisciplinary study, written or oral communication, or participating in learning communities. Indeed, nothing in the course description suggests the development of the expertise associated with professionals. The definition of teaching supported by this seminar is limited to its being a "job."

Indeed, the language of this description primarily focuses on the teacher, on graduate students becoming "comfortable" in their role as teacher. It is the teacher functions of organizing discussions, negotiating relations to the material (and the senior professor), managing office hours, designing activities, and pacing the course that is the subject of this seminar. Rather than the language of care of the student/client seen in the historical documents of the last chapter, or the Boyer report's more carefully worded attention to the learning activities, Michigan's seminar puts the teacher at the center of the course.

In Rutgers University's English Department, there is a different kind of teaching seminar description. For fall 2002, Kurt Spellmeyer taught the department's "Teaching Writing" course required of first-year teaching assistants. Spellmeyer's description reads:

> Today, when the field of "English studies" has started its second century, it is easy to forget that writing courses were among the very first that English professors taught. In

many ways, however, composition still supports the entire edifice of English. By a large margin, more undergraduates take courses in composition than they do in any other area of study, and this demand for writing instruction had made it possible for English departments to maintain, over three or four generations, large graduate programs with resources for many TAs [teaching assistants]. Far from diminishing recently, with the declining humanities job market, the importance of composition continues to grow. As of 1996, composition is the largest single division in the MLA. Composition is taught more widely, and by more professors, than any other course in the English curriculum. It is also the most rapidly expanding field of specialization, with the largest number of new positions every year since 1985.

Composition has always played a central role in the institutional history of English, yet it has developed a distinctive intellectual tradition, with concerns that differ in important ways from those of literary study. This "tradition," theoretically and practically, is the subject of 552, which will be organized under three headings: (1) the construction of literacy; (2) the production of discourse; and (3) the politics of knowledge and education. It is important to understand that composition as a field starts with literacy rather than with literature—its concern is anthropological rather than aesthetic or philosophical. It does not try to determine how books should be read but how various kinds of reading have in fact been socially constructed. In this same anthropological spirit, compositionists start with "discourse" rather than with "text"—they start, in other words, with the social sites that enable and constrain literate practices. And this concern with social sites has produced, in turn, a conversation about the ways in which knowledge operates to preserve and disrupt long-established structures of authority.

Xeroxed readings will be supplied by Dr. Spellmeyer

each week. Work for the course will include short response papers in addition to two longer (10 page) papers integrating our readings with classroom practice. (Spellmeyer)

A comparison of Spellmeyer's course description to others in his department makes the long historical introduction he provides to this course seem less unusual and more in keeping with apparent department constructions of the genre. Still, notice the different emphasis in Spellmeyer's course from the one taught at Michigan. Spellmeyer clearly identifies historical and institutional forces that are a part of the practice of having graduate students teach the introductory composition course and a set of disciplinary areas of expertise—literacy, discourse, and politics of knowledge and education. While we cannot know much of the specifics of the readings or the activities Rutgers's graduate students are expected to complete during this course from this brief description, it is very clear that the construction of teaching has moved away from the practices and comfort of the new teacher that were key features in the University of Michigan course and toward the political and institutional forces involved in teaching. Furthermore, the work graduate students are expected to do for the teaching seminar course at Rutgers is much more like that done in other graduate seminars—papers, both short and long. The subject of Spellmeyer's course, then, is neither the teacher nor the learner, but the cultural construction of the composition course as an institutional requirement.

A third example taken from the University of Nebraska at Lincoln demonstrates another version of the required teaching seminar. The version for fall 2002 reads:

Aim: This seminar is required of all graduate students during their first semester of teaching in the English Department. It has four related aims: (1) to explore several theories of teaching and language (with emphasis on writing and reading), (2) to help teachers develop, sharpen, and articulate their own theories of teaching and language, (3) to aid teachers in designing reflective classroom practice consistent with those theories, and (4) to sponsor a vision of teaching—and specifically the teaching of writing—as a site of scholarly work. Using our own classrooms as research labs, we will explore the dynamic and dialogic relationship between theory and practice.

Teaching Method: Discussion (sometimes student-led), activities, student presentations.

Requirements: Several projects that ask students to connect theory and practice, including the creation of an assignment sequence, a (text)book review, a teaching philosophy statement, and a classroom research project. Students who enroll for four credits will also participate in one of several out-of-class discussion groups (one hour per week).

Tentative Reading List: As a graduate seminar, this course asks students to read widely in the field and to write regularly in response to that reading. Our tentative reading list includes Anson et al.'s *Scenarios for Teaching Writing*, Amy Lee's *Composing Critical Pedagogies*, and a packet of theoretical and practical articles on teaching and language. We will also inspect program materials from UNI's first-year writing program. Teachers who know they will take this course are invited to nominate articles for the packet of readings. (Gallagher)

In this version of the teaching seminar, the multiple roles such a course plays are made more explicit, and the forms of writing required of students taking the course are related to both the genres they encounter as teachers (assignment sequence), as future candidates for academic positions (teaching philosophy statement), and as teacher/researchers (a classroom research project). Such a preparation invites prospective teachers to see their work in the classroom not only as a set of practical concerns (as at Michigan) or even a collection of historically and politically constructed ideologies and practices (as at Rutgers) but as potential sites of scholarly investigation and knowledge making.

My point in offering these examples is not to suggest that one of these teachers of teachers is clearly better than the others; indeed, each of these courses may be an improvement (or not) over prior versions of the course. They may also very well be all that the local politics and interests of the moment will allow. It is clear, however, that these versions of required teaching courses are imagining *teaching* and what is important to those beginning to teach very differently. But the Boyer report fails to distinguish that there can be such differences. Because the commission lists its suggestion so simplistically, it seems to endorse any kind of course no matter what its structure or underlying conception of teaching, learning, or undergraduate education might be. In fact, the report seems to ignore what at least some commission members must have already known: that teaching seminars are now quite common in English departments that employ graduate students to teach the introductory composition courses, and yet those courses are neither equally rigorous nor sufficient to alter practices or conceptions that devalue teaching in those departments.

The difficulty, of course, is that a single seminar cannot begin to provide the intellectual foundation necessary for making fully informed curricular or pedagogical choices required of those who would purport to be "professional" teachers at the university level. Most of these pedagogical seminars are required as a condition of employment rather than as a part of the degree requirements, and this condition further compounds their lack of status. The telling phrase in the Michigan description is "to the job of teaching assistant," an indication that the course is not conceived of as a part of the graduate degree program but rather as a condition of employment. The "issues" covered in the course are thus not issues of teaching that concern all faculty, but rather the issues of teaching assistants, issues that need not be revisited once the doctoral degree is obtained and the graduate student assumes the role of becoming a professor, it is the expertise one has gained as a scholar that dominates one's actions rather than any "training" one has had to work with students. The Boyer report's use of terms such as *training* and *apprentice*, and its justification for attention to teaching on the basis of employment patterns has done nothing to upset this tradition; indeed, much of what it says and fails to say reinforces the very practices it seems to wish to disrupt.

Thus, while the language and institutions are no longer so overtly gendered, teaching is still connected to direct work with students: the job one does before being fully authorized to join the profession. And, on becoming a professor, it is the expertise one has gained as a scholar that dominates one's actions rather than any "training" one has had to work with students. The Boyer report's use of terms such as *training* and *apprentice,* and its justification for attention to teaching on the basis of employment patterns has done nothing to upset this tradition; indeed, much of what it says and fails to say reinforces the very practices it seems to wish to disrupt.

Reforming Status

There is another contradiction that runs throughout the entire Boyer report but is particularly visible at this moment when the preparation to teach is the center. Focusing on the need to reform research universities is a strategic move that the commission explains early in the document: research universities are the pinnacle of higher education in this country even though they educate a tiny fraction of the undergraduate population. The statistics on the first page summarize the picture quite well. While research universities account for only 3 percent of all higher education institutions, they award 32 percent of the undergraduate degrees. Research universities also have a disproportionate influence on decision making across industry, education, and government. Because research universities prepare most of the professors who go to work at other institutions of higher education, changes at research universities will eventually spread to other schools. Starting reform with research universities adds the weight of prestige and status to good example and ought to ensure a more widespread adoption of the positions being advocated. But this argument about the influence of research universities coexists with an argument that research universities have a unique mission centered on research, the making of knowledge; research universities, the report argues, "must facilitate inquiry" even among undergraduates.

Inquiry-based learning rather than the passive reception of knowledge is the first and central reform advocated by the commission. It is a reform that is easy to support for those who have become comfortable in the postmodern discussions of constructed knowledge, praxis, and epistemic rhetoric. But it is hard to see why such an education ought to be limited to students at research universities or how it can be contained there once the influence of these institutions spreads the reforms to other schools. If research universities are truly the one place where such learning can happen, how does preparing all graduate students to understand their role in the classroom as "promoting inquiry" actually prepare them to address the missions of and students at nonresearch institutions unless the mission of all institutions of higher education are similar, at least for undergraduates?

The commission report specifically argues against the attempts to replicate the small liberal arts at the much larger research universities. It also criticizes the "nip and tuck" approach at reform already undertaken at many institutions when what is necessary is "radical reconstruction" (Boyer Commission 6). But having framed the report as a call for radical action uniquely appropriate for research universities, the recommendations are actually neither particularly radical nor reasonably limited only to research universities.

Finally, the Boyer report's list of recommendations for "educat[ing] graduate students as apprentice teachers" mixes items that attend to material conditions with items that speak to professional education. Having time to adapt to graduate school before taking on the responsibilities of teaching, for example, is a matter of the economics of funding graduate study through teaching assistantships that employ graduate students to teach undergraduates. Likewise, compensating teaching assistants with a living wage or, as the commission puts it, to "reflect more adequately the time and effort expected," is clearly an issue of material conditions. Teaching graduate students to promote learning by inquiry, however, goes directly to the intellectual preparation to teach, to what might become the definitions of sound pedagogical practice and appropriate undergraduate education.

Unfortunately, merely juxtaposing economic features of the work of graduate student teachers with ideological positions that could be used to define professional standards does not by itself redefine what counts as professional education. Instead, the recommendations appear to give universities and even individual departments a choice of equally valid options for educating graduate students as apprentice teachers; some of those ways involve providing more money to individual graduate students, an economic reform that cannot be equally available to all institutions. Most, probably all, of the recommendations could be adopted without significantly rethinking the relationship between teaching and research or the epistemology underlying classroom work.

Indeed, even the language of "apprentice" echoes the work practices of the early guilds rather than an intellectual or professional history. Could we imagine, for example, calling for graduate students to be educated as "apprentice scholars"? Of course graduate students are still learning to be scholars; who among us isn't? Few would advocate, however, that graduate programs should be satisfied with producing a scholar who might function as an apprentice rather than preparing fully authorized, independent scholars. All the rituals of a doctoral degree—from qualifying exams through the oral defense of a complex and unique act of scholarship—are meant to authorize a colleague, not an apprentice. To suggest that graduate students be prepared to teach because they must do so as professors places the material conditions of university life at the forefront, but it does nothing to realign the division between teaching and scholarship nor does it argue for teaching as a legitimate intellectual enterprise. The status of research has not been altered by this report, and teaching is most definitely not being professionalized.

The next chapter demonstrates how these efforts to improve the material conditions of teaching produces another pattern of discourse inherited from the past, an inheritance that has undermined the professional status of teaching for at least a hundred years.

4 / A Mere Factory Hand

The 2001 National Council of Teachers of English publication *Moving a Mountain: Transforming the Role of Contingent Faculty in Composition Studies and Higher Education,* edited by Eileen Schell and Patricia Stock, poses this question on its back cover: "How can the academy improve the working conditions of those who teach most of the core curriculum in higher education today: part-time and non-tenure-track faculty?" The question, like the collection of essays it frames, echoes another historical pattern in the discourse surrounding the professionalization of teachers: a concern for the material conditions of teaching.

One historical figure with similar concerns was Margaret Haley, a founder and key figure in the Chicago Federation of Teachers. In 1904, when Haley gave a speech before the National Education Association entitled "Why Teachers Should Organize," she included four conditions of teaching that, she argued, could best be addressed by unionizing for collective action. Those four included:

1. Greatly increased cost of living, together with constant demands for higher standards of scholarship and professional attainments and culture, to be met with practically stationary and wholly inadequate teachers' salaries.
2. Insecurity of tenure of office and lack of provisions for old age.
3. Overwork in overcrowded classrooms, exhausting both mind and body.
4. And lastly, lack of recognition of the teacher as an educator in the school system, due to the increased tendency toward "factoryizing education," making the teacher an automaton, a mere factory hand, whose duty it is to carry out mechanically and unquestioningly the ideas and orders of

those clothed with the authority of position, and who may or may not know the needs of the children or how to minister to them. (148)

I have more to say about Haley's efforts to alter the conditions for classroom teachers at the beginning of the nineteenth century later in this chapter, but, for the moment, note simply the recurring concern for material conditions of teaching. Here, then, is my next claim: the difficulty inherent in these discussions is the tension between the values associated with professionalism and the organized structures of bureaucracy. Once those discussions reach higher education, the tension is compounded by the long-standing distinctions between scholarship and teaching.

Scholars of various fields, including English studies, have taken up both professionalization and bureaucracy; the connections of both to labor issues, especially unionization; and the histories of professional organizations and institutions without providing a clear resolution to the tension those of us in higher education, particularly in composition, experience on a daily basis. Although I do not pretend to have the answer that has escaped so many others, I am prepared to make this further claim: we need to recognize the traps created by the discursive patterns we inherit and work to conscientiously construct alternatives if we hope to improve either the material conditions of classroom teachers or the relative value of teaching within the structure of higher education.

To illustrate my contention that concern with material conditions of teaching re-creates discursive patterns that are both historic and unlikely to provide solutions to the dilemmas of current higher education, I begin with a series of scenarios that have arisen in my current life as the director of a composition program that employs graduate students in English and non-tenure-track (NTT) faculty to staff its more than one hundred sections of composition each term. While some of these stories and the issues they raise are representative of higher education in general, my effort here is to focus on the specific site of composition programs, the site I know best and with which readers of this series are most concerned. I know that others would represent the events I am about to relate differently and that the very activity of committing these events to the page is an interpretive act. I have tried, however, to create these scenarios as completely as I can so that readers can consider them in relation to their own experiences. I do not believe anyone involved in these events acted in bad faith or that there are easy and obvious "sides" to be taken in the issues they raise. Indeed, it is through the explication of the complexity usually hidden within such scenarios that I intend to illustrate the intellectual dimensions of teaching and that of the administrative work that is usually dismissed as merely service, dimensions that are regularly undertheorized. It is precisely the undertheorizing of both teaching and writing program administration that have kept (and will continue to keep) efforts to improve material conditions of teachers, or attempts to take teaching and programmatic development seriously, from having a significant impact on the values or structures of higher education.

Scenario 1: Maternity Leave

One of the lecturers in my program applied in May for maternity leave for the fall term. She gave birth in late June and received a letter from the dean and associate provost for faculty affairs shortly afterward responding to her request for paid leave. The letter asked for clarification of her request because the maternity leave policy would give her ninety days following the birth, thus requiring her to return to work at the end of September. Since she could not be assigned to a class midsemester, she could return to assume non-teaching duties that I, as her supervisor, would determine—duties such as tutoring in the writing center, the letter suggested—or she could take unpaid personal leave for the remainder of the term. Since tenure-track (TT) faculty women had been given maternity leave for the whole semester within the previous year, and since the department had fought an extended battle over maternity leave for a postdoctoral student classified as "staff," not "faculty," only a few years previously, the decision represented what seemed to be a new policy, one that reduced faculty benefits to the level previously consigned only to staff. Finally, it was a policy that had not been announced prior to this attempt to implement it. Apparently, however, meetings had been held with deans from the various colleges, the university's legal counsel, and the provost's office to define a practical and fair policy. One concern for the university was that faculty members from various departments and colleges, and even different campuses, be treated equally; thus, individual chairs or supervisors ought not devise accommodations on a case-by-case basis without the guidance of a clear policy.

As the direct supervisor in this case, I was concerned for several reasons. First, I wanted to treat this faculty member humanely; she taught well, had contributed significantly to the program, and, in fact, had just been renewed for a second three-year appointment. Second, I knew that the faculty member was trying to be realistic about her ability to balance mothering newborn twins and another preschool child with the considerable time and attention she gave to her teaching; I wanted to foster the kind of professional judgment I saw her exercising. Third, I knew from my own experience directing a writing center that no one can do forty hours (our full-time equivalent) of tutoring each week (even without newborns). Furthermore, it was not at all clear how much documentation of productivity was implied in the suggestion in the letter that I could determine other nonteaching responsibilities "subject to the Dean's approval."

I also worried about this decision from a policy perspective. Is it really good long-term policy to have people believe that the university is unreasonable or insensitive? Policies that privilege short-term economics over the well-being of individuals seem to merely encourage attempts to manipulate the system and convince individuals to stay quiet rather than be forthcoming about plans that may affect a program. Given the large number of contingent faculty in our program, I am particularly sensitive to the very real possibilities of their exploitation. Any policy that fosters distrust, I would argue, is shortsighted and likely to make everyone's life more difficult. Furthermore, in an institution that is trying to "improve conditions for women," is it good policy to make maternity leave more difficult to take or disconnected from the realities of teaching on a term schedule?

Perhaps, I worried, this was really a way of treating NTT faculty differently from "regular" faculty and thereby, once again, devaluing both contingent faculty and the teaching they are hired to do. Were department chairs going to be asked to work out nonteaching duties "subject to the Dean's approval" for tenured or tenure-stream faculty members who requested such leave? For tenure-stream faculty, who, of course, earn more than contingent faculty, taking an unpaid leave and stopping the tenure clock might not seem much of a sacrifice. In fact, continuing to serve on department or university committees, counseling graduate students, advising undergraduates, and working on scholarship without reentering the classroom midsemester could easily constitute "nonteaching" duties and still fit into the life of a new mother. But, since teaching faculty do not have defined research or departmental duties other than teaching, how could they really return "full-time" to duties that are not usually a part of their job description? In our composition program, at least, there are various recognized administrative duties, and, as it happened, I had no one filling those roles at that moment. Thus, I could assign administrative work to this faculty member, letting her work on a flexible schedule, and, because of her experience and past performance, I was certainly willing to do so in her case. Would I be so willing to trust such work to others who might be in the same situation later? What would happen if more than one person were to request leave at the same time? Since there are no recognized administrative duties for lecturers who teach in the literature or creative writing programs in our department, was it fair to establish a policy that would work in one program, at least some of the time, but would not be feasible in other areas even within the same department? How was the directive to devise other nonteaching duties for this faculty member consistent with the bureaucratic concern for rules that could be applied equally across all cases? Was the fear of possible litigation actually creating a situation that could lead to legal action because policy would only obscure the real practices? Finally, even at a procedural level should the policy not have been announced in advance, discussed in open meetings like the faculty senate or the collegewide faculty meetings, and subjected to faculty vote before being applied to the faculty members who happened to be making the request this year? In the words of one chair, we were witnessing policy creation by "administrative stealth," a situation that could not be tolerated by faculty committed to shared governance even if we agreed to the policy itself. Ironically, though, even if the policy were discussed at such faculty meetings, NTT faculty are not invited to participate and do not have representation in the faculty senate.

To complicate the matter further, the administrators who made this decision do not consider themselves nonfaculty. In fact, like most universities, administrators at my institution rise from faculty positions to serve for a few (or many) years as deans, provosts, and even vice presidents before returning to their departments full-time. All administrators with faculty status at my institution teach classes on a regular basis and continue their efforts to publish and present their scholarship. Finally, since financial resources are always limited, do faculty and administrators not have a responsibility to consider the fiscal ramifications of policy decisions and to make choices among various priorities? Is it better, for example, to offer full-semester maternity leaves for the handful of faculty who would make use of such a benefit or to address the inadequacy of other faculty benefits like salaries, support for attending professional conferences, or paid sabbaticals prior to tenure? Thus, if taken before the faculty senate or voted on by all the eligible (read TT) faculty, would maternity leaves (semester-long or not) be awarded to NTT lecturers?

As it happened, a TT faculty member in a different department received a similar letter, and department chairs were able to insist collectively that the policy be discussed and approved before being applied to these particular cases. Both women received the full semester leave with pay awarded to others in prior years. The following spring, the faculty senate approved a revised parental-leave policy providing paid "work load relief" to all TT faculty and to any full-time NTT faculty who had completed 24 months of service to the university if they were the primary caregivers (Green "Parental Leave").

Scenario 2: Hiring Full-Time Lecturers

Like many other universities, mine has struggled with the financial benefit of using NTT faculty and the problems inherent in doing so. The department has long argued that a better program and better teaching will come from employing teachers full-time rather than part-time and giving them a living wage with benefits. Significant pay raises have occurred in the last few years for full-time NTT faculty, and such positions have been added regularly to the composition program as enrollments demonstrate growing stability. The numbers are worth mentioning: twelve full-time lecturers at $26,000 in 1999 with no merit-raise percentage increase possible and limited to three years maximum; twenty-eight lecturers at a starting salary of $30,500 with merit increases possible for each year of service and the possibility of reappointment beyond three years in 2002.

Furthermore, the tenure-stream faculty in my department take teaching seriously even if they are not always in agreement about what constitutes "good" teaching, how to recognize it, or how to document it so that it can be rewarded. Tenure-stream faculty have the added pressure to produce significant scholarship. Rather than give up the hard-won teaching load of two courses a term in favor of more lower-division teaching or collapse small discussion courses into large lecture formats, TT faculty in my department are pressured to cede responsibility for the first-year composition courses, and even many of the introductory literature courses, to NTT teachers. Most are also genuinely caring people who see their own graduate students struggling to find employment in a tight job market.

They hope that a few extra years of teaching full-time will help these younger scholars find a workable life or allow them to bide their time until the job market opens up. The largest increase in the number of full-time lecturers came in the spring of 2001. In response to a faculty senate decree that either three or four classes would qualify as "full-time," the administration decided to convert the positions that had taught a three-course load, known locally as "semester lectureships," into full-time positions with a four-course load. Semester lecturers were appointed only for one term at a time, but because these positions carried benefits, they were significantly better than the usual part-time status even though the pay rate was a set rate per course. Full-time lecturers, on the other hand, cost the university significantly more because they were paid a salary in addition to benefits, were guaranteed employment for the full school year, but taught only one course more each term than semester lecturers. Some part-time faculty (paid per course but without benefits) would still be necessary, but their assignments would be limited to no more than two courses each term. For the composition program, this meant nine new lecturers in addition to the renewals we were already scheduled to open up for a search. Word of the final changes did not come, however, until the hiring committee had already met to consider the first wave of applications, and the exact number of new positions was not determined until the final moments of the process.

Because my department has required that NTT faculty hired to teach composition demonstrate professional commitment by assuming various programmatic duties, composition lecturers have always been included on the hiring committees considering new appointments. Such democracy is not, however, university or even college policy. In fact, treating NTT faculty the same as tenured and tenure-stream faculty makes some people in higher education very nervous. The faculty senate does not represent NTT faculty, and the faculty handbook, written by the faculty senate, prohibits NTT faculty members from making hiring decisions about faculty.

When it became clear that the large number of positions created by the conversion of semester lecturer positions into full-time positions would make a national search desirable, I requested funds from the dean to have members of the hiring committee attend CCCCs, where we could conduct interviews. The dean initially denied funds on the grounds that NTT faculty could not participate in the decision-making process without violating senate rules unless the department voted to give them such authority in this situation. The department promptly did so, though perhaps without fully understanding the ramifications, and a composition lecturer got to spend her spring break at the conference interviewing candidates and attending sessions.

More than eighty individuals applied to our position advertisement, many with significant experience in the classroom. Only one, however, had a doctorate in composition and rhetoric, although several had literature doctorates in hand or were in the process of completing their dissertations (ABD). Some of those with literature degrees wrote eloquently about their commitment to teaching and their scholarly work in various areas; few provided teaching materials that demonstrated how they taught writing. Many of the applicants had M.F.A.'s and were actively producing fiction, nonfiction, and/or poetry. Several applicants had worked in editing, publishing, or journalism. A few had high school teaching experience and a handful of candidates had their master's degree in composition and rhetoric or in teaching English to speakers of other languages. We also had, not surprisingly, several internal candidates from the pool of part-time faculty who had been working in the department for years. Some of the candidates, employed already or not, had degrees from the department.

As the committee members read applications and interviewed candidates, they found that those candidates who could articulate their approaches to teaching writing in concrete terms quickly rose to the top. Whether they referred to particular theorists, or any theory, mattered less to the committee than that they conveyed an interest in, and some strategies for, teaching writing to first-year students. A pool of acceptable candidates emerged and the committee set about deciding on priorities among them. The best choices were easy to identify and quick to place at the top because their qualifications and experience were so visible. The second tier, though, was harder to rank-order precisely because they were all "acceptable" for different reasons; some of us had favorites because of particular aspects of the files and our sense of programmatic needs, but all of us could argue the strengths and weaknesses of individual candidates and arrive at different rankings.

Among that second tier were several internal candidates, some of whom were also being considered by a separate departmental committee hiring lecturers to teach the introductory literature courses. Because introductory literature courses are classified at the sophomore level, lecturers must have a doctorate in literature to qualify for this assignment; a master's degree in "English or a related field" is acceptable for teaching composition even though composition instructors are also responsible for advanced courses at the junior level and literature lecturers never teach outside the sophomore level.

As these separate committees wrestled with how best to arrive at final decisions, some members of the literature committee seemed to be lobbying for the composition committee to hire internal candidates who had been teaching literature in the department for several years, freeing the department to hire "new blood" for those positions, but ensuring that these former students would continue to have full-time work that accommodated their personal lives. At the least, these literature faculty members argued, the composition committee should reveal its rank ordering of candidates so that their committee could decide whether they needed to continue to consider these local candidates. After all, they argued, both committees were a part of the same department. These suggestions seemed to the tenured faculty member on the composition committee to be totally out of line. The NTT faculty members were not approached with these suggestions or requests. However, at least one member of the literature committee apparently suggested later that NTT faculty should not be making these decisions because they could be controlled by the director. When I abided by our committee's decision to keep the rank orders confidential until we had firm acceptances for all positions, I was accused of being "uncooperative" with the department.

That a single department had two different committees hiring different kinds of NTT lecturers with different minimum qualifications is indicative of both the widespread division between composition and literature and the more local history of lecturers hired to teach composition migrating into literature assignments. The dean insisted that the assignments had to be kept separate; someone hired to teach composition must teach only composition, and part-time personnel should teach literature courses not covered by full-time faculty. Given the interests of the candidates, the difference in pedagogical demands, and the difficulty of attracting qualified candidates from outside the immediate area, especially for teaching literature, such a strict division seemed to most of us in the department not to be in anyone's best interest.

A final aspect of this scenario is the disappointment of those not hired for these few positions. Some seemed to assume that length of time in the classroom was the only qualification that ought to be considered, and, unable to accept the loss of benefits or the public rejection in competition with others who would become their new colleagues, they refused to continue as part-time faculty. The elimination of benefits has also altered the makeup of this particular group of faculty members. Of the eleven faculty who worked less than full-time the composition program employed in 2000–01 school year, seven were men (64%). In 2001–02, we initially planned to employ seven such faculty members, but we ended up with additional temporary conversions when it proved impossible to find qualified candidates willing to work without benefits. We also lost candidates to the literature program because of their preference for teaching literature. Thus, we entered the fall term with only four part-time faculty members, two men and two women. The percentage of full-time instructors in composition, however, confirms what is known about how heavily gendered by female bodies the field really is. Our total percentage shifted from 53 percent to 75 percent female with the additional full-time lines.

Scenario 3: Faculty or Graduate Student

The fall term was about to begin when I received a call from the dean's office asking whether one of our recent hires was also a graduate student in the department. It seems that over the summer, the chair of the faculty senate had written a letter to the deans of the college and graduate school pointing out that the faculty handbook prohibits graduate students in a department from simultaneously being faculty. Likewise, spouses of graduate students are not allowed to have faculty positions in the same department. English was singled out as a regular violator of this policy, but the senate was willing to not "initiate action" against those with current positions. Unclear from the letter, though, was whether this agreement to ignore current candidates "inappropriately hired" would apply to these individuals once their current one-year contracts ended or was to extend indefinitely (Green "Pursuing").

As tenured faculty members began to hear the story, they recognized immediately the impact such a policy would have on doctoral students who were not finished with their degrees when their teaching assistantships ended. These faculty members insisted that the language of the handbook had never been interpreted to apply to NTT positions before. Indeed, several longtime faculty members insisted, the policy had been created at a time when some departments were hiring their own graduate students into TT positions before they finished their dissertations. Those practices were clearly a conflict of interest, but hiring ABDs as lecturers was simply not the same my colleagues argued. Besides, why would it make sense for the composition program, for example, to be able to hire an ABD from the history department to teach composition, but not be able to hire a similar candidate from English? Why would it be acceptable to hire an ABD in English from elsewhere, but not be able to offer such an opportunity to our own doctoral candidates? The faculty senate simply needed to change the handbook to say that graduate students still pursuing a degree in the department could not be hired as "regular" faculty in that department. The question of whether faculty senate had the *right* to create regulations affecting

NTT faculty when it denied such faculty membership or voting rights was an issue few seemed to be interested in raising.

Scenario 4: Let Them Have Buses

It was late in the convention, early in the morning, and I was tired from too much talk, but I made my way to the open business meeting at the 2001 CCCC convention anyway. Years ago, my master's director insisted I go with her to a similar meeting at NCTE and I have been going to such meetings every year, usually with friends in tow, because she was right: you learn a great deal about your professional organization, the issues, and the key figures in the field from such occasions. That particular year I arrived a bit late, but in plenty of time to settle in before Ira Shor rose to make a motion with an appropriate preamble of rationale. Given the surplus in the organization's coffer, he said, and given the interest in making space for all the teachers of composition at our annual meetings, $50,000 should be set aside to hire buses that would transport part-time faculty members from major cities within four hundred miles of Chicago to the following year's conference. The motion was quickly seconded, but several people rose to speak against it.

How would buses limited to a four-hundred-mile radius help those contingent faculty who lived in other parts of the country, teachers more likely to find the distance to the conference an obstacle to their attendance? Was spending so much money really fiscally responsible? How could the audience asked to vote know? Would it not be better to direct the executive committee to investigate ways to support conference attendance, but leave the amount and the means up to those who could study the ramifications more carefully? Since part-time faculty are not always the only ones in need, the former CCCC president Cynthia Selfe reasoned, why not amend the motion to include any member in poverty? Was transportation even for those within four hundred miles really the expense that kept people from being able to attend? Would the money be better spent on airfares for those who lived farther away, or perhaps on hotel vouchers for contingent faculty? Better yet, why not let people decide for themselves how best to use the funds the organization could offer to defray the costs to individuals by simply offering scholarships to attend. Buses seemed to smack a bit of patronizing the have-nots; at that pre-September 11 meeting, no one could imagine tenured faculty members taking a bus instead of catching the commuter flight from mid-America. Should the money be limited to those who were presenting papers and so acknowledge the professional commitment of contingent faculty, or was the intent to get people professionally involved and add new members to the organization in the process by offering a financial incentive to attend the conference? Would such efforts really increase attendance or membership of the targeted group, whichever group that might be? Could we even agree on the objective of such a large expenditure?

And so the discussion went, with numerous suggestions for "friendly amendments," but only one—that an additional $50,000 for special scholarships for adjuncts whose proposals were accepted on the program—agreed to by Shor. Numerous people rose to argue that the organization seemed unwilling to put its money where its mouth was, and to remind us of the dire conditions for NTT faculty by describing their own sacrifices and miserable economic situations. After much debate, and a vote in support of the motion that required several executive members to walk the perimeters of the room counting raised hands, more speakers rose to explain why they could not vote for the motion even though they supported the efforts to improve the conditions of NTT faculty. Someone pointed out that a motion from the floor was only advisory in any case, and the executive committee would have the final say. Others were indignant that anyone, even an elected body as carefully constituted to represent all the geographic and institutional divisions of the organization as was the executive committee, would counter the will of the group that had assembled that morning and had already voted.

As I listened to this debate, I was remembering the series of sessions a small group of us had organized for this very convention on the problems women in our field were having getting tenure on the basis of their work with beginning teachers, including graduate students and adjuncts. Several of us had been in that position: denied tenure despite publications, outstanding teaching, and considerable administrative contributions to our departments and programs. Our situations were unique, refracted as they had to be by our different careers, the institutions in which we worked, and the personalities involved, but we were all women committed to a view of intellectual work that integrated our work as teachers, teacher educators, or program administrators with our publications. We had made our professional commitments to the field visible in our lives, and we had been denied the final gold star of legitimacy represented by gaining tenure. Our professional organization, despite such structures as the Commission on the Status of Women, seemed oblivious to our condition. Of course, we had all gone on to other TT jobs, and perhaps in the end we would be fine, stronger for the struggle and wiser from the process. Our panel presentations had generated large audiences and support from several well-known figures in the field. The patterns of our experiences suggested there was more to these episodes than random individual cases, but no one had called for unified, professional action.

I scribbled a motion of my own: that the executive committee convene an ad hoc committee or otherwise investigate the role the organization might play in cases in which tenure had been denied to those members of the profession, particularly women, who had enacted nontraditional views of intellectual work, including administering programs, preparing teachers, or running writing centers. When the debate on buses finally stopped, I read my motion with the caveat that I would be happy to elaborate if necessary, but that in the interest of time would refrain from doing so since I thought the necessity for the motion was obvious. My motion passed in a voice vote with no discussion and no apparent opposition.

Six months later, the executive committee had set aside $25,000 to support attendance and participation at the annual conference by those who would not be able to attend for financial reasons, agreed to spend half of the executive committee November retreat discussing a "Professional Equity Project," and directed the incoming chair to oversee implementation of this project. No action had been taken on the motion regarding tenure and promotion for those with nontraditional career profiles (Samander). At the 2002 conference in Chicago, the incoming president had no idea of the status of the motion to support women gaining tenure and promotion, and no memory of it having been discussed when asked what action the executive committee had taken. Though one might argue that "professional equity" could reasonably include the gender inequities that appeared to underlie the tenure denials for those of us enacting nontraditional views of intellectual work, the outgoing president could only say to me that she had "dropped the ball."

I cannot give the final resolutions for these scenarios since each of them is only a moment in an ongoing story. Even if I could provide the final outcome of each case, my purposes for this project are actually better served by simply presenting these scenes as indicative of the complexity and undertheorizing, that permeates higher education's discussions of faculty, material conditions, and reevaluating teaching and institutional work. In the rest of this chapter, the tensions these scenarios invoke will be unpacked in order to illustrate and prove the claims made earlier: that current discussions of material conditions in higher education are repeating historic patterns that are inflected by class, gender, and long-standing divisions between scholarship and teaching, between literature and composition. I examine two sets of oppositional terms that underwrite these discussions: *professionalism* versus *bureaucracy* and *scholarship* versus *teaching*. In each pair, I am interested in the repetition of discursive patterns that employ assumptions about gender, labor, and teaching that survive "from a time now dead."

Professionalism versus Bureaucracy

Philo Hutcheson's 2000 book on the American Association of University Professors (AAUP) provides a clear summary of the difference between professions and bureaucracies:

> A profession exhibits five characteristics: 1) It has exclusive powers to recruit and train new members as it sees fit.

2) It has exclusive powers to judge who is qualified. 3) It is responsible for regulating the quality of professional work. 4) It has high social prestige. 5) It is grounded in an esoteric and complex body of knowledge. . . .

The bureaucratic organization is a means of assuring clients that judgments are based on technical criteria rather than personal ones and that all members of the organization participate in hierarchical relationships of authority. While bureaucratic employees can develop areas of expertise that allow some autonomy, they nevertheless work within the boundaries of specific technical rules and under contract to organizations. . . . The characteristics of professionalization, especially autonomy, expertise, and the lack of specified work rules, are in obvious contrast to bureaucratization. (4, 6)

Since faculty in higher education are professionals because of their scholarly disciplines, Hutcheson argues, but members of a bureaucracy because of their employment within institutions, they have always struggled with these contradictions. Other professional groups (like doctors) have only more recently come to experience these same contradictions (via the controlling bureaucracies of hospitals and health maintenance organizations, for example). Indeed, as Hutcheson's tracing of AAUP history makes clear, university professors have a long tradition of distancing themselves from labor unions in order to maintain their status as professionals.

In the initial call to organize the AAUP in 1914, for example, the comparison to the American Bar Association and the American Medical Association "in kindred professions," makes professional organization the clear intent of the founders. Likewise, the concern that the organization not be relegated to the status of a labor union is made clear in statements like this one from H. W. Tyler, a former general secretary of the AAUP who wrote in 1938:

The Association is not a "Professors Union." The epithet, many times thoughtlessly rather than ignorantly applied, might be fitting if the Association had devoted itself to protecting the economic rights and increasing the monetary rewards of its own members, or perhaps of restricting their performance. (qtd. in Hutcheson 14)

Tyler's characterization of "professors union" as an "epithet" makes it obvious that such a label was not positive. His justification for insisting that the AAUP was not a "union"—that the organization had eschewed economic rights and monetary rewards in favor of other professional issues—serves to define the distinction between unions and professional associations centered on economic benefits. Even as the AAUP became involved in collective bargaining in the mid-1960s, it did so with considerable reluctance and calls for a noninindustrial model of labor-management relations more befitting the shared governance of professionals. President Fellman, firmly against the association's involvement in collective bargaining, is reported to have remarked in 1965 that the decisive issue of that year's convention was not a case of academic freedom but "whether we should convert into a trade union" (Hutcheson 73). The following year, Fellman's annual address insisted that:

> Of course we defend the right of professors to join a trade union if they so desire, and we are strongly opposed to the imposition upon them of reprisals of any sort for so doing. Nevertheless, our Association is not a trade union, it is not part of the trade union movement, and it does not seek that identification with organized labor which trade union status would imply. (qtd. in Hutcheson 94)

In a working paper on the issue presented at this 1966 convention, the arguments for and against various versions of collective bargaining were considered. Among the negatives, the report listed the loss of identity as a professors' association because the membership criteria would have to change to include NTT faculty who had to be a part of the bargaining unit at many institutions. The report also recognized a significant difference between shared authority represented by traditional governance structures of higher education and "polarity between employer and employee" engendered by collective bargaining (Hutcheson 140). Although the report argued that both the traditional values of the organization and the actions of collective bargaining were equally important, two dissenting reports were attached that argued otherwise. For these members, the AAUP had to stand for a "high view of an academic *profession* and for a concept of the university as a community of scholars and not as a corporation that employs teachers" (qtd. in Hutcheson 141).

This reluctance to concede the status of a professional organization in order to take up collective bargaining representation at local institutions was so strong that the organization actually only became formally involved in collective bargaining by accident. In 1967, without notifying the national office in advance, the faculty at a small, two-year college in Illinois elected the AAUP as its representative rather than choose the American Federation of Teachers (AFT), which represented the local public school teachers. Once involved, AAUP leadership continued to expect that collective bargaining would be an issue only in two-year colleges at which the faculty followed patterns more like those in secondary schools than the "professional approaches that characterize higher education" (Hutcheson 121).

Hutcheson does not try to investigate why university professors would have such an aversion to unionization, but it is hard to miss the opposition established between professional and labor, or the professors' desires to distinguish themselves from public school teachers. A quick look at the cultural context and history of teacher unionization makes the discursive pattern that distinguishes university professors from classroom teachers, and professional organizations from labor unions, apparent.

Classroom Teachers as Laborers

At the end of the nineteenth century, industrialization, urbanization, and an influx of immigrants made city schools ripe for reform. As demonstrated in chapter 2, classroom teachers were frequently the target of reform efforts that employed the language of professionalization even though the reforms rarely provided teachers with the education necessary for them to make professional decisions and seldom distinguished between experienced teachers and those who wished to become teachers. For many classroom teachers, these attempts to privilege college degrees over experience with children, to divert attention away from the physical conditions of schools and to ignore the low wages of the predominantly female classroom teachers all in the name of reform were efforts that had to be resisted. One site of resistance was Chicago, where Margaret Haley led the Chicago Teachers Federation (CTF), a precursor of the AFT.

Haley's involvement in resisting administrative efforts began in 1900, when the Chicago School Board claimed it did not have enough money to pay teachers the raise they had been promised. During the Christmas holidays, Haley did some investigative work looking at tax records, and what she found led her to take a leave of absence from teaching in order to help with a legal suit challenging the tax breaks given to utilities and big businesses in Chicago. The suit eventually brought nearly $600,000 of back taxes into the city. By the time it did so, Haley was working full-time for the CTF and had to seek an injunction to force the city of Chicago to use the money to pay teachers instead of raising the pay of firefighters, police officers, and janitors (Haley *Battleground* 79–81).

A savvy participant in Chicago politics, Haley recognized, perhaps more than any other educator of her time, the importance of the social and political structures within which teachers were asked to do their work. She knew, for example, that funding made a difference because such material conditions of teaching as class size, resources, length of day, and building conditions made a difference in the lives of children and teachers. She seems to have known instinctively that a teacher being moved outside the neighborhood where she lived and/or had worked mattered not only because it caused her inconvenience and increased her living expenses without increasing her pay, but because, as Marjorie Murphy's 1990 study of early teachers' unions would demonstrate, such centralization destroyed a teacher's ability to know her students well, connect to parents, and draw on community resources. Moving outside her home neighborhood also altered a teacher's position as a leader in the community; in other words, it changed the way she could function even as it changed the conception of her role.

But as Haley undertook the work of improving these conditions, she seems to have become ensnared in the language that kept her from claiming these concerns as professional issues and left her instead with the language and actions of labor. At the beginning of her career as a teacher, Haley had traveled to summer institutes featuring such educational theorists as William James and Colonel Francis Parker. When she moved to Chicago, she had joined a teaching circle to read and learn about such subjects as cognition, child development, and pedagogical theory. Despite these earlier interests in additional education, Haley's later writings argued for teachers to stop "running like hares to classes which give them nothing but promotional credits" and instead study "the real problems of our country," "learn the essentials of money, land, and taxation systems," and then teach these to their students (Haley *Battleground* 272). Such language was seen by educational leaders at the time as an indication that Haley (and by extension the teachers' unions) not only resisted further intellectual development but were also willing to misuse the classroom to advocate a political position. Since overt political behavior in the workplace was seen as contrary to the behavior of professionals, Haley's words were used against her as proof that teachers were not professionals and needed to be reformed through further education and closely supervised by those who would behave as professionals, that is, as apolitical.

Furthermore, Haley officially connected her organization to that of Chicago's American Federation of Labor (AFL) until a decision by the school board in 1916 to fire any teacher belonging to a labor union forced her to sever the ties between the CTF and the AFL. The school board and leaders of the NEA like Nicholas Butler argued that labor activity was unprofessional because it advanced personal welfare over the conditions of the professional's client, in this case the student. Haley's attempts to counter this criticism did not successfully negate the accusation that the CTF was self-serving. In her 1904 speech before the NEA, for example, she claimed that:

> There is no possible conflict between the interest of the child and the interest of the teacher, and nothing so tends

to make this fact evident as the progress in the scientific conception of educational method and administration. For both the child and the teacher freedom is the condition of development. The atmosphere in which it is easiest to teach is the atmosphere in which it is easiest to learn. The same things that are a burden to the teacher are a burden also to the child. The same things which restrict her powers restrict his powers also. (146)

Haley's argument, as is seen in this passage, is structured as a series of parallel assertions without example or supporting detail. For those members of her audience who already accepted these assertions, such as the classroom teachers who joined her in the CTF, these linkages must have been obvious, but for the leadership of the NEA, Haley was not convincing. When she follows this paragraph with a description of the difference between professional organizations and unions, she perhaps unwittingly supports the very distinction that the educational administrators controlling the NEA were claiming:

The element of danger in organization for self-protection is the predominance of the selfish motive. In the case of teachers a natural check is placed upon this motive by the necessity for professional organization. The closer the union between these two kinds of organization, the fuller and more effective is the activity possible to each. (146)

In acknowledging both the danger of selfish motives inherent in unionization and the necessity that teachers be professionals, Haley makes room for an argument that teachers should belong to professional organizations and shun union agendas. Haley may have intended that the professional organization would take up the issues of material conditions, but, by separating the two kinds of organization, she re-created the very opposition she most needed to unite. By 1918, the year after the court ruling in support of the Chicago School Board's Loeb rule dismissing teachers who belonged to labor unions, the NEA had launched a campaign to get every teacher in the country to be a member as a "professional duty." In a climate of war that demanded outward signs of loyalty, membership in the NEA, required by many superintendents across the country, rose from 8,466 in 1917 to 87,414 by 1920 (Murphy 91).

Several forces combined to link teaching to labor rather than to profession for Haley and other early teacher union leaders. First, women did not have the right to vote and Chicago schools were controlled through an elected school board and the personal influence of the local aldermen. Schools, at least in Chicago, were vehicles of political power, and getting things done required political connections. Joining with labor unions gave the mostly female classroom teachers the vicarious voting clout necessary in their politicized world.

Chicago's climate of corruption at the turn of the century is well known, and nowhere is that corruption more visible than in the histories of the Chicago public school system. Leaders of the NEA and public criticism like that generated by Joseph Rice's exposé on urban schools in 1892–93 argued that incompetent teachers got and kept their positions only because of this political corruption that allowed aldermen to bestow such favors. Murphy's book argues, however, that while aldermen could appoint teachers to schools, these teachers kept their positions only by demonstrating to their principals and the superintendent that they were capable. The real corruption in the schools, Murphy suggests, was in the misappropriation of funds for such routine items as coal and in the awarding of contracts and inflation of costs associated with the building construction required by an ever increasing urban population.

A second force that seems to have contributed to the CTF's aligning with labor is the almost invisible hand of Chicago's elite in reforming the city's schools. The Chicago Commercial Club, an exclusive gentlemen's club, was known for its systematic involvement in civic affairs, for example. It seems only natural that teachers objecting to the reforms designed by club members would seek allies in those who were already opposing the activities of these industry owners and managers, and who was more in opposition to industry management than the labor unions? Likewise, when President Harper of the University of Chicago set out to pass legislation to centralize the Chicago school system and require a college degree for teacher certification, he turned to the women's clubs for support. The teachers lobbied successfully against this bill, known as the "Harper bill," causing its defeat first in 1899 and then again in 1901, 1903, and 1909. Murphy reports that even though the women's clubs generally supported the idea of school centralization, the antiwoman language in the Harper bill made their involvement much more tempered than the activities of women's clubs in New York, where Nicholas Butler was successful in passing similar legislation (Murphy 28–29). Nonetheless, Murphy reports that Chicago teachers were suspicious of the women's clubs' attempts to lobby them with afternoon teas, and that Haley later characterized the club women's 1895 opposition to a teachers' pension bill as an example of their "caring for their maids better than schoolteachers" (Murphy 29). Given the predominance of working-class and immigrant women in teaching at this point, such comments are surely indicative of a class consciousness that would support closer affiliations with workers than with industry leaders or reformers.

A further indication of this split in the education community along class lines is visible in an 1894 resolution that arose from the floor at a NEA meeting. The resolution offered by the Texas Teachers' Association is recorded as follows:

> Whereas, For several years our social equilibrium seems to be very unstable, strikes and other evidences of dissatisfaction upon the part of one class in opposition to another class; and
>
> Whereas, There is a wider and deeper estrangement between those who labor with their hand and their brain against those who labor more particularly with their brains alone; and
>
> Whereas, The estrangement has grown into open defiance of the rights and security of property, and even to bloodshed; therefore, be it

Resolved, That it is the sense of this Association, the duty of the teachers of this state to at once enter upon a systematic course of instruction, which shall embrace, not only a broader patriotism, but a more extended course of moral instruction, especially in regard to the duties of citizenship, the right of property, the security and sacredness of human life.

Resolved, That this Association request the National Association to take up this subject, and that, too, with a full realization of the responsibility that the education of the children of this country is virtually in the hands of the schools, in the hands of 500,000 teachers, who should teach 25,000,000 pupils what they wish to appear in these children when they become citizens in order to perpetuate our common country—our free republic. (34)

Although the language of this resolution seems to current day readers to be fairly even handed, it was not voted on immediately but referred to the resolutions committee composed of five members and rewritten with a much more overtly proindustry slant before being approved. The rewritten version reads:

The National Educational Association has assembled at a time of marked public disturbance and of grave industrial unrest. The highest powers of the nation have been invoked in time of peace to enforce the orders of the courts, to repress riot and rapine, and to protect property and personal rights. At such a time, we deem it our highest duty to pronounce emphatically, and with unanimous voice, for the supremacy of law and the maintenance of social and political order. Before grievances of individuals or organizations can be considered or redressed, violence, riot and insurrection must be repelled and overcome.

Liberty is founded upon law; not upon license. American institutions are subjected to their severest strain when individuals and organizations seek a remedy for injustice, fancied or real, outside of and beyond the law. We call upon the teachers of the country to enforce this lesson in every school-room in the land, and we heartily accept and endorse the suggestion transmitted to us by the Teachers' Association of the state of Texas, that upon the schools devolves the duty of preparing the rising generation for intelligent and patriotic citizenship, by inculcating those principles of public and private morality and of civil government upon which our free Republic is based, and by means of which alone it can endure.

We heartily commend the wisdom and firmness of the President of the United States, as exhibited in this trying time, and we pledge to him and his associates in the conduct of the government our hearty and enthusiastic support in the enforcement of law and the restoration of order. We must, at the same time, record our perfect confidence in the capacity of the American people to grapple with any social problems that shall confront them. Riot, incendiarism and conspiracy are not native growths, but have come among us by importation. They cannot long survive in the clear air of American life. (34–35)

Particularly noteworthy in the rewritten resolution is the shift from supporting "a broad patriotism" and "moral instruction, especially in regard to the duties of citizenship" to the "supremacy of law and the maintenance of social and political order." Patriotism thus becomes limited to allegiance to laws and the status quo rather than to encompassing a range of activities and duties connected with individual citizens. Also overt in the revision is the blaming of immigrant groups in the last paragraph for the disruptions that require teachers to take action. Apparently, the NEA leadership, despite its criticism of teachers unions' politicized activity, thought it appropriate for teachers to instruct students in political and ideological ways as long as that instruction supported the government and industry leaders.

A third factor leading teachers to use the language of labor rather than a language indicative of professional ideology is the association of professionals with advanced learning. For teachers already teaching, and for those of limited means, one of the reasons to oppose legislation like the Harper bill that centralized schools and set standards for teacher certification was the requirement that teachers have a college degree. The CTF argued that the cost of additional education was unlikely to be recovered in higher wages for female teachers, and the education offered by universities, like Harper's own University of Chicago, was not necessarily useful to their activities in the classroom. Instead, when teachers were required to attend extra classes beginning in 1905 in order to qualify for a pay raise, they went to free classes at the Art Institute to demonstrate their willingness to gain further knowledge. The superintendent, however, refused to acknowledge these as legitimate courses and denied the pay raise (Murphy 30). Further education was apparently not the issue for either the teachers or the educational establishment, but controlling that education certainly was. Control, or at least resistance to the control of managers, was an activity labor leaders understood and could impart to classroom teacher unions.

Finally, using the language of labor to describe the desires and problems of classroom teachers was the natural outcome of being denied the language of professionalism. As demonstrated in chapter 2, women's opportunities to participate in professional organizations, even when they were the majority of the profession's members, were severely limited in the nineteenth century because of the ideology that made it improper for women to assume a public role. Although Haley tried to work within the NEA and had some success in making a larger space for women and classroom teachers' concerns there, the NEA leadership remained firmly in the hands of the superintendents and college presidents. The organization's executive council refused to appropriate money to study salary issues, for example, and the new charter of 1919 successfully sidestepped the vote of the membership and created a delegate assembly that essentially disenfranchised the more unionized urban teachers (Murphy 98–99).

Haley was not, or course, responsible single-handedly for linking teaching to labor. Indeed, this construction permeates the discourse at numerous sites and continues to pit professionalism against unionization in current discussions as well, though it is not always recognized as the heart of the disagreement. Take, for example, the turmoil generated within the MLA over the 1995–96 grade strike by graduate students at Yale. Yale graduate students, organizing for better pay and health benefits, aligned themselves with an AFL group that also represented the institution's cafeteria workers, then went on strike and refused to submit grades for the fall term. The administration would not negotiate with this group, saying that it would only work with an elected graduate student organization other than the Graduate Employed Student Organization (GESO). The teaching assistants who failed to release grades were fired. At the December meeting of MLA, the delegate assembly supported the students and passed a resolution condemning Yale, but by the time the resolution arrived in members' mailboxes for their vote, it was accompanied by five letters of opposition written by Yale faculty who were MLA members. In the letter written by Yale faculty member Annabel Patterson and sent to the MLA membership, the controversy was represented this way:

> The university administration, whose leaders are all Yale faculty, has consistently refused to recognize [GESO] as a "union," not only because it does not believe this to be an appropriate relationship between students and faculty in a nonprofit organization, but also because GESO has always been a wing of Locals 34 and 35 of the Hotel Employees and Restaurant Employees International Union, who draw their membership from the dining workers in the colleges and other support staff. Yale is not prepared to negotiate academic policy, such as the structure of the teaching program or class size, with the Hotel Employees and Restaurant Employees International Union. Yale administrators have made it perfectly clear that they have no objections to working with an elected graduate student organization

other than GESO, one that is not tied to the nonacademic unions on campus. (qtd. in Bérubé 158)

Michael Bérubé characterizes Patterson's use of quotations around the word union as "scare quotes," and perhaps they are. But it seems equally possible that Patterson was drawing attention to the problem of constructing faculty members, in this case graduate students, as workers rather than professionals, and the disjunction created when the striking teachers were labeled graduate students, members of a labor union, or professional faculty. Patterson's elaboration of the academic issues that the administration does not want to discuss with a nonfaculty union is a further example of the historic tension between labor and profession. In this historic distinction, faculty (professional) status is required in order to participate in the shared governance surrounding academic issues, but the hierarchical relationships of the bureaucracy are sufficient to negotiate employment (labor) practices. In fact, Bérubé himself points to this tension without fully explaining it when he says:

> At the very least, then, the grade strike muddied the question of whether the job actions at Yale were matters of labor relations or of academic protocol: if they were the former, then Yale was clearly involved in illegal union busting; if the latter, then striking GESO members were clearly abrogating one of their primary obligations as undergraduate instructors by failing to turn in their grades. (155)

Although Bérubé is not using the term *professional,* the values of professionalism—specifically the responsibility of the professional to act in the best interests of the client—are implied in Bérubé's linking "academic protocol" to "obligations as undergraduate instructors." Since the issue, as Bérubé structures it here, is one of "labor relations or of academic protocol," it appears to be impossible for activities in protest of material conditions to be those of a professional, even for Bérubé.

Let me be clear. I do not disagree with Bérubé's suspicions about how the MLA ballot mailing was tainted by the inclusion of explications and justifications for only one side of this argument. Nor do I think Bérubé wrong to notice that administrative positions in academic institutions, like those of managers in other businesses, have a predilection against labor issues. But I do hear in Patterson's letter an echo of the historic insistence that university professors are professionals and therefore cannot behave like labor and maintain their status. If graduate students are members of the faculty because they teach classes, then their actions will engender the kind of responses from some other faculty, even faculty administrators, that the Yale students encountered. Bérubé's insistence on emplotting the debate as a traditional Marxist narrative in which the downtrodden and oppressed do battle against oppressive administrators and conservative faculty simply does not help to explicate the forces at work in such recurring contestations between material conditions and professionalism, between the scholarship that gives TT faculty authority and the labor of classroom teaching that defines those not (yet) on the tenure track. Nor can such a rendering be of much use in reimagining what it means to be a university professional/professor.

Of course, there is much suspicion, sometimes even disdain, among academics for the traditional claims of professionalism. As recounted in the first chapter, many academics want to distance themselves from "professionalism" because of its associations with claims of objectivity and client interest even though economic benefits and class privilege coincide with professional status. But as Stanley Fish has argued, such an antiprofessionalism stance relies on the critic's own desire for the professional value of individual merit and is thus itself an example of professional ideology. Furthermore, the sympathies of many scholars informed by Marxist-inspired study lie with workers in ways that are also influenced by self-interest. Indeed, as higher education has opened its doors to a broader spectrum of Americans and university professors have expanded to include many from working-class origins, the historic tension between *professional* and *worker* has come to be an internal dilemma for individual professors as well.

Some features of the scenarios that begin this chapter can surely be understood as examples of this tension between professionals and workers. The privileges assigned to faculty members and denied to NTT faculty or the reverse privileging that offers support money to NTT faculty and denies it to other faculty members who may not be any more financially secure are already scripted on the basis of assumptions about individuals' professional/worker status. Still, the professional versus bureaucratic worker dichotomy that aligns with distinctions between academic concerns and material conditions within higher education at both institutional and individual sites cannot fully account for the complexities of the scenarios with which I began.

Scholarship versus Teaching

In introducing the collection of essays on the Yale strike, Cary Nelson writes:

> Universities persist in claiming graduate students teach as part of their doctoral training, not as employees, even though higher education is pervasively dependent on cheap instructional labor, with graduate assistants, postdocs, adjuncts, part-timers, or a mix of the above teaching exactly the same introductory courses on campus after campus. In the case of graduate teaching assistants, many of whom teach fifteen to twenty-five courses over six or seven years, the learning curve peaks years before the work ceases. (25)

What Nelson does not say, perhaps because his audience already knows it, is that those classes that are the same from institution to institution are, for English departments, primarily courses in composition. Nelson is right in suggesting that graduate students teaching as part of their "doctoral training" is something of an institutionalized lie since there is little evidence that graduate programs structure these assignments in ways that would support such a claim. As illustrated in chapter 3, the preparation to teach given to graduate students in English departments is (and for a century has been) inconsistent, disconnected from the preparation they receive for scholarly independence and expertise, routinely criticized as ineffective and insufficient, and frequently devoid of the intellectual preparation that would give these beginning teachers the expertise of professionals.

But Nelson's statement is also indicative of the tension between scholarship and teaching; can we imagine suggesting that the "learning curve" for scholarship peaks before the work is over especially for those who are productive enough to publish fifteen to twenty-five articles in six or seven years? The assertion that there is little to be learned but much to endure in teaching—especially in composition teaching—is, of course, a commonplace in English departments. In fact, Nelson's statement is almost an exact replication of a report by a 1952 CCCC committee which observed: "The teaching of composition is often regarded as an apprenticeship leading to 'good courses,' and the teacher is likely to get a feeling of diminishing returns after a few years, compared to his experience in teaching literature" (Griggs 10). Likewise, John Brereton demonstrates how prevalent this lack of intellectual engagement in teaching is in his review of the recent memoirs of three university teachers who clearly had successful careers but write of their own dissatisfaction with and even alienation from their work in the classroom (Brereton "Careers").

Furthermore, although the "cheap labor" Nelson outlines is performed, as he acknowledges, by various kinds of teachers, it is only "graduate students" who are qualified in the final sentence as being unable to learn more from the activity of teaching. Nelson's concern for graduate students casts them as rivals of others who teach these same courses. In Nelson's construct, these others are merely teachers and apparently deserve to be cheap labor because they are not bright enough to become bored with such assignments or do not have aspirations to become scholars via the graduate study that leads to a doctorate. Unfortunately, even in composition and rhetoric programs in which teaching and teacher preparation are typically taken very seriously, a close review of the available data raises questions about the way teaching assignments are constituted as a part of graduate education.

The *Rhetoric Review* 1999 survey of doctoral programs in composition and rhetoric lists the various criteria used to assess suitability for academic study as: goals and purpose statements, letters of recommendation, GRE scores, graduate and undergraduate grade point averages, and writing samples (Brown and Jackson). More than half of the programs surveyed considered the goals and purpose statement and the perceived fit with the program as the number one criteria for admission. All sixty-five programs reviewed list teaching assistantships as the first source of financial aid, but only seventeen consider teaching experience as one of the six listed criteria for admission into the program. Of those seventeen, only three —Indiana University of Pennsylvania, Arizona State, and Purdue— list teaching experience as one of the top three criteria considered in the admissions process. In fact, once admitted to a program, teaching assistantships are more likely to be awarded to candidates on the basis of "scholarly promise" than because of teacherly promise or evidence of teaching competence. Likewise, the best students in any program are often candidates for funding that does not include the responsibility of teaching. Such practices construct teaching first as "work" (a way to earn money), not a part of the professionalizing process of graduate education; second, as inferior work, requiring no expertise and little or no training (while anyone with enough intelligence is qualified to teach, the most promising intellects would be wasted in teaching); and third, as devoid of intellectual interest (teaching does not contribute to graduate education because it is not a site of knowledge making, only knowledge transference).

Since more than half of the programs reviewed in the *Rhetoric Review* survey state that teaching assistantships are available to "all" graduate students, and sixty of the sixty-five list first-year composition as the primary course taught by teaching assistants, we might reasonably expect that these programs would include extensive preparation to teach. Unfortunately, as pointed out in chapter 3, written descriptions of the procedures used in individual programs to prepare TAs to teach are incomplete and problematic. It is common for departments to have some kind of orientation prior to the first teaching assignment. In addition, most programs have at least one required teaching seminar. However, many of these institutionalized efforts to prepare teachers take a decidedly practical perspective, emphasizing not the intellectual issues underlying teaching but the tips of classroom management, bureaucratic record keeping, or program conformity. The names of the courses themselves are revealing: "Teaching Practicum," "Teaching Workshop," "Teaching Laboratory," or, my favorite, "Introduction To Teaching," though there never seems to be anything to follow the introduction. In contrast to the qualifying exams required before advancing to the final stage of doctoral work, I have located no articulation of an equivalent assessment of teaching competency necessary for advancement or graduation from a doctoral program in English, even a doctoral program in composition and rhetoric.

Finally, what little attention there is to preparing graduate students to teach, or to think of themselves as teachers, is focused on teaching composition. Teaching seminars are often linked to teaching a required first-year composition course in order to "earn" the teaching assistantship that funds graduate study. Such seminars are almost always taught by faculty members in composition, often by junior faculty. As in the examples examined in chapter 3, teaching seminars are frequently required of all teaching assistants "new to the department" or of entering graduate students who have never taught before. Graduate students who enter programs without assistance in the form of assistantships are routinely prohibited from enrolling in these seminars, and students who enter a program with a similar course from another institution are frequently exempted from the pedagogy seminar even if they would like to enroll.

Fall orientations are likewise commonly designed and led by those in composition, sometimes with the help of graduate students or adjuncts. That such practices mean that composition faculty routinely have at least one week less of summer to devote to their publications than do other tenured and tenure-stream faculty members is rarely acknowledged. Since most of us in composition are indeed interested in teaching, these assignments may seem only natural; we are, as Joseph Harris so aptly reminds us in his 1998 book, "The Teaching Subject" of English studies. But who among us does not recognize the disadvantage of having to teach a required course? A course that is often emptied of our scholarly expertise precisely because it is required for those employed to do a particular job? A course that counts as our graduate course for the year, but that is frequently reduced to fewer credits, and thus less time, than the standard graduate seminar? A course that our colleagues who defend our work at tenure and promotion discussions have to explain and defend to faculty from other departments that do not require such an introductory seminar for their graduate student TAs? A course, finally, that has little chance of establishing the relationships between faculty and students that departments do value—the relationship of scholarly adviser or dissertation director?

Indeed, embedded in these routine practices of English departments are a number of discursive links that constitute teaching, even (perhaps especially) the teaching of teachers, as work; as "women's work;" as nonintellectual work. For example, upper administration is likely to agree to support a seminar specifically connected to the "job" of teaching a required course like composition. Such a course can be justified as helping to ensure consistency between multiple sections of a required course and as improving student retention rates because this required course would be better taught if the teachers are prepared for it. Such a justification is consistent with the requirements of bureaucratic consistency and impersonal decision making; it does not call on the language of professionalism by suggesting that graduate students need to gain expertise before being allowed to make the multiple decisions required of classroom teachers or that the profession would not endorse the omission of such a course from a degree in English. In fact, when such courses are taken along with the first teaching assignment in the department, they do not function as preparation at all, but rather as support and supervision mechanisms in a hierarchical bureaucracy. University administrators may not even be asked to endorse such a requirement because it does not require their financial support and, in fact, generates full-time equivalent funding. Once the teaching seminar course has been justified as "job training," it can also be dismissed on these same grounds as not worth the same amount of attention from students as other graduate courses. For many departments, the lesser value is signaled with fewer credits or less time. Even when the standard three credit hours is awarded for teaching seminars, the expectation is that a teaching seminar "lessens" the burden on beginning graduate students because the course is "practical" rather than theoretical and rigorous.

The practices surrounding teaching seminars, and the justifications that accompany their required status, whether explicitly stated or not, serve to gender teaching as feminine. Teaching is work, a part of the bureaucratic structure rather than the structure of the profession of academic scholarship; it is intellectually empty, requiring no particularized study prior to entering the classroom because it is inborn, as "natural" as mothering was said to be for females in the nineteenth century; it is a part of an apprenticeship, a childlike step toward becoming the adult scholar, and requires only attentive modeling of the masters. Since composition carries the full weight for preparing and employing graduate students as teachers in most English departments, it is further feminized within higher education even if the individuals occupying these positions are not themselves female.

Of course, many in the field of composition inhabit female bodies as well. Studies have repeatedly shown the predominance of women in composition classrooms (for examples, see Enos; Holbrook; S. Miller; Schell). Sue Ellen Holbrook estimates two-thirds of those who teach writing are women, for example. But these same studies also establish a larger percentage of men publishing in key journals and dominating theoretical—as against nurturing or pedagogical—research categories (for a succinct summary of this data, see Miller *Textual Carnivals* 124). It is doubtful, however, that all the women teaching composition have degrees in the field. In fact, given the glut of doctorates in literature and the willingness of most departments to hire those with master's of fine arts or master's degrees to teach introductory courses, determining exactly who occupies the large number of lecturer positions is difficult. Creative writing degrees, and master's degrees in composition, rhetoric, and technical writing, which would serve to qualify candidates at many institutions for part-time lectureships, but not TT positions, are earned primarily by women. Women earn 60.8 percent of the degrees in creative writing and 72.8 percent of the composition-related master's degrees according to the National Center for Educational Statistics (NCES Table 257). As more institutions turn NTT lines into full-time positions, the distinctions represented by national statistics categories like "full-time faculty" will be even more difficult to interpret.

It is easy to establish, however, that doctoral degrees for women in all fields have risen steadily throughout the twentieth century, and that in English more women than men have earned doctorates each year since 1980–81. The most recent statistics are for 1997–98, when 59.12 percent of the doctorates in English were awarded to women (NCES Table 287). A breakdown of the focus of these degrees, however, reveals that the vast majority (74 percent) were in general language and literature, and 79 percent of those degrees were earned by women. Meanwhile, the degrees in composition, rhetorical studies, and technical writing combined (representing only 8 percent of the total doctorates in English) were more evenly distributed (52 percent were earned by women) (NCES Table 257). Thus, it might be reasonable to find more NTT positions held by women if TT positions reflected the overall gender distributions of area specialization. In other words, we would expect more women to be hired for TT positions in English in general and the gender balance in TT composition and rhetoric positions to be more equal.

The MLA's Committee on the Status of Women in the Profession reports a drop in TT positions for both men and women from

1992 to 1997, but women have fared worse in this trend than their male counterparts. In 1992, a year when 59 percent of the doctorates in English were earned by women (NCES Table 287), 52.8 percent of these women landed TT positions (MLA Committee on the Status of Women in the Profession 194). In 1997, women earned 58 percent of the doctorates and only 32.8 percent found TT positions that year. For men, the drop in TT positions went from 49.6 percent to 37.7 percent in the same time span. Men were more likely to turn to positions outside higher education (12.3 percent of the male graduates took such positions in 1997, compared with 9.9 percent of the women). There has also been a greater tendency to hire recent women graduates for NTT positions. In 1992, 34.2 percent of the new female graduates entered NTT positions, but, by 1997, 47.5 percent of the new female graduates took NTT positions. Male recent graduates entering NTT positions climbed from 36.4 percent in 1992 to 39.1 percent in 1997 (MLA Committee on the Status of Women in the Profession 194).

Returning to *Rhetoric Review*'s survey of doctoral programs and analyzing the data provided about core faculty members in these programs reveals the following. In the 62 programs reviewed, a total of 432 faculty members could be identified by gender on the basis of unambiguous first names. The gender balance overall is, indeed, reflective of the balance in degrees awarded in the field (51 percent of the positions are held by women, compared with 52 percent of the degrees awarded). There is, however, a somewhat troubling pattern in the breakdown by rank: 22.45 percent of the total positions are held by men who are full professors, compared with women full professors, who hold only 12.5 percent of the total positions. Male associate professors account for 15.2 percent of the total, while female associates account for 20.6 percent. Male assistant professors account for 8.56 percent, compared with female assistants at nearly twice that, 16.2 percent. Nonranked positions are virtually equal at 1.85 percent men and 1.62 percent women.

While the data provided by the *Review* is problematic for a number of reasons (it is out of date by the time it is published; unable to reflect recent promotions, moves, and hiring; relies on self reporting by each program; includes faculty who might not have degrees in composition and rhetoric themselves; and excludes graduates who take positions in programs that do not offer the doctorate in the field), it is one of the only sources of gender distribution by rank currently available, and the only one that separates composition faculty from other fields in English. The data seem to suggest that women stay at the associate professor rank longer than do men, and/or that hiring women in the field for doctoral programs is a more recent phenomenon. A third possible explanation of this data is that more women are denied tenure at such institutions and move into positions in departments that do not grant doctorates in composition and rhetoric, an interpretation that is supported by the anecdotal evidence revealed in the series of panels on women in the field at the 2001 CCCC conference.

Thus, the statistical data further support what has long been claimed: that teaching and composition are both heavily gendered "women's work." What is even more telling, however, is that not only are the ranks of NTT classroom teachers occupied by women who probably do not have degrees in the field of composition studies, but the field itself, despite its almost equal appeal to men and women, has supported men in their career advancement more successfully than it has supported women, even when the growth in doctoral programs has allowed an increased number of TT positions in this area.

These practices, like Cary Nelson's statement about graduate students learning all there is to know about teaching long before the work stops, reveal the deeply held assumptions about teaching and scholarship that define university professors' work. Lionel Lewis's book *Marginal Worth: Teaching and the Academic Labor Market* argues that because teaching and service are tied to local contexts they cannot be valuable commodities for academics; only research, because it is both portable and measurable by outsiders, can be leveraged in the academic marketplace. Richard Miller is equally blunt when he argues that composition and rhetoric, because of its interests in teaching first-year students and in preparing teachers, can never be a "discipline that can compete with other disciplines"

("Writing" 247). Miller's arguments about the institutional value of programmatic efforts in composition, the need for waging rhetorically savvy arguments to improve material conditions for classroom teachers, and the futility of language that constructs composition teachers as slaves, or teaching in general as dependent on romanticized passion, are indeed insightful. He repeats, however, the fundamental error of dismissing the intellectual dimensions of teaching, insists that teachers ought to avoid "persist[ing] in thinking of the work we do as a vocation rather than a job" (243), and he urges those in composition to become adept at bureaucratic management. Scholars like Miller and Lewis would have us believe that since teaching and composition have been constructed as devoid of the expertise or independent judgment of professionals, composition teachers, whether TT or not, can only band together to forge strong programs that allow the teacher-workers to be measured against known programmatic standards like other laborers. In such a view, TT program directors have few choices to assuage the guilt about their own mixed status as professors who function as bureaucratic managers than to do as Miller suggests: leverage the service of doing work others do not want to do (teaching first-year students and teaching teachers) into better conditions for these workers. Of course, as long as these program directors are men they appear to have a much better chance of being rewarded for such work than do their female colleagues.

Not everyone is as quick as Miller and Lewis, however, to dismiss the intellectual dimensions of teaching. Ernest Boyer and Lee Shulman, largely through their work with the Carnegie Foundation, have made such phrases as "the scholarship of teaching," "making teaching visible," "teaching portfolios," and "preparing the future professoriate" commonplace in current discussions of higher education. For Shulman and others like him, teaching can be evaluated like scholarship if it is made visible so that other members of the profession can evaluate it. Thus, Lewis's comments that scholarship is portable because it can be evaluated by outsiders is merely a description of the current state of affairs, not an absolute feature of these professorial activities.

The difficulties individuals and institutions have encountered trying to enact these arguments for reconsidering the distinctions between scholarship and teaching are numerous, however. Much as we might want to agree that teaching could be portable, could be valued more, could be made visible and thus subject to evaluation by outsiders, some of the impediments to doing so stem from the language even these scholars use to reconceptualize the relationship of teaching and scholarship. For example, Boyer argues that repositioning faculty activities as falling along four different but overlapping areas of scholarship would help erase the distinction between research and teaching. Those four areas of scholarship include

- discovery (adding to human knowledge);
- integration (making connections between disciplines and between disciplinary communities and the larger world);
- application (interactions between theories and practices); and
- teaching (transmitting, transforming, and extending knowledge to others, including other scholars). (Boyer 15–26)

These areas of scholarship allow for the possibility that publications might be acts of teaching, but classroom work or interactions with students are not easily positioned within the other categories.

Likewise, despite the best efforts of many thoughtful educators, efforts to "make teaching visible" have frequently created demands that teaching be made to look like scholarship. For example, in tenure review and in hiring, requesting teaching portfolios has become routine, but how those portfolios are to be read and evaluated is all too often treated as self-evident. Teachers who want to suggest that their classroom practices are integrated with their publications (another site of an intellectual project rather than merely a place to tell students about their scholarly expertise) must create extra documents explaining their teaching practices because the usual documents of teaching (course syllabi, assignments, or comments on student work) are not usually read for the threads of the intellectual project being advanced. In other words, these teacher-scholars cannot rely on common understandings of genres or be certain that their readers already understand how to read these pedagogical documents. Producing more than is customary in a given situation, however, also runs the risk of being misread. As I explained in my article on the politics of representing the work of directing a writing center as part of an intellectual project, institutions that do not expect such materials to be presented during the tenure review can easily dismiss them as service, consider them signs that the candidate is trying to compensate for inadequacies of "real" scholarship, or imagine that the productivity they represent could have been used more fruitfully in traditional publications (Marshall 81–84).

Likewise, the request for a teaching portfolio from job applicants or for consideration of a teaching award regularly produces little more than a random course syllabus that is clearly written to give students operating rules but not necessarily a sense of the course or the teacher's work. Evaluators who expect a teaching portfolio to demonstrate the applicant's conception of teaching, mastery of common practices, and interactions with students find themselves wondering in such situations how they are to sort unqualified candidates from those who merely have not learned to consider how to represent their teaching to outsiders.

Tenure-track faculty who have taken Boyer's call to recognize the "scholarship of teaching" as an invitation to center their publications on pedagogy have frequently been relegated to the margins when older, more traditional faculty interpret such publications as less serious, less scholarly, indeed, "merely pedagogical." Boyer's own separation of "teaching" as a distinct category that includes but is not limited to publications seems, in fact, to isolate the pedagogical focus from the other areas of "discovery," "integration," and "application." Readers might reasonably question how "discovery," once it takes a written or oral form that allows others to share in the discovery, is not an act of "teaching." If courses integrate or apply knowledge, for example, do they not become—like the publications in Boyer's schema—"teaching"? And, if teaching is the overarching or underlying category, how did Boyer think representing it as a separate unit of the four types would alter the hierarchies of higher education or stop the forces that pit teaching in opposition to research?

Another example of this problem of undercutting the intention to reconsider the relative worth of various activities of faculty in higher education appears in the MLA Commission on Professional Service. This commission, formed in 1992 to address the imbalance of the reward structures in higher education for faculty activities, argued for a reconceptualization away from traditional research, teaching, and service with research clearly on top and service expected but ignored. Instead, the commission suggested, faculty should be evaluated and rewarded for contributing to a matrix of academic values that include both intellectual work and academic and professional citizenship in different sites (MLA Commission on Professional Service 162). While the commission kept research, teaching, and service as the three sites of faculty work, its attempt was to articulate how different activities in each site could represent intellectual engagement. The commission argued, for example, that teaching must be recognized as involving more than merely direct contact with students in classrooms, and as being "practiced at high and low levels of intellectual investment" (164). Likewise, relegating all activities that are not research or classroom teaching into the category of "service" does not differentiate between perfunctory tasks and those that involve considerable intellectual expertise and commitment.

Where the commission undercuts its own arguments is in treating research, teaching, and service as three separate sites for academic work and in plotting specific examples of faculty activities in the grid comprising these sites and values. Such a visual representation reinscribed the very divisions the commission argued discursively are inappropriate. In addition, appearing to position different work, like training TAs or editing a journal, as firmly located in particular categories and at particular places in continuum, contradicts the commission's own recognition that any faculty activity is inflected by the local conditions that constitute that work and the faculty member's own intellectual engagement and reason for participating. It is quite possible, in fact, to find examples of training TAs that are neither teaching nor intellectual work but rather the citizenship activity of institutional support. Surely, it is also possible for such an activity to be a centerpiece of a faculty member's intellectual agenda, representing all the characteristics the commission identifies as essential to intellectual work: "rigor, skill, care, intellectual honesty, heuristic passion for knowledge, originality, relevance, aptness, coherence and consistency" (163).

If the commission had instead suggested that intellectual work and academic citizenship could be evaluated against accepted values (such as originality, innovation, quality, consistency, collaboration, growth, and timeliness) and that sites of faculty work include those within particular institutions or organizations as well as those outside these employment and professional structures (i.e., the public community), they would not have been able to plot specific activities within the matrix. The commission's representation of faculty work would have been more consistent, however. Furthermore, it would be reasonable for specific institutions to define other values or to require specific sites of faculty activity in assessing tenure and promotion cases, but it would not be reasonable to omit whole categories or values, or specific activities, from the reward structure. Thus, over time, individual faculty members ought to be expected to produce written work addressed to both the internal and the external communities in which they work, to produce both formal scholarship and informal assessments or reports, and to make new discoveries in both written and enacted forms. They could be expected to teach in a variety of formal classes, in one-to-one contacts like tutoring in writing labs or serving as dissertation readers, and in less structured settings like cross-disciplinary committees on which their expertise is essential to the task at hand. Faculty might be asked to serve on committees that advance the work of the department, college, or professional organization and on some that are intimately connected with their own academic projects. They could be expected, in other words, to articulate exactly how their various activities have advanced both their own intellectual projects and the professional settings in which they function.

My argument, then, is not that the commission was wrong, but that, like the Boyer report, it did not go far enough in insisting that faculty activities be evaluated and measured by articulated criteria representing the intellectual engagement of professional teacher-scholars. Of course, both of these groups functioned within a complex, political setting that required choices and compromises. The MLA commission explains its decision to keep the research, teaching, and service categories "for the sake of continuity and maximum usefulness, in part because classification in these categories still exerts such an enormous influence on the way faculty work is perceived and valued" (172). Such a rhetorical compromise is understandable, especially when the commission goes on to suggest that it wishes to "redefine" these terms. But, like the Boyer report, these rhetorical compromises leave the reformers trapped in constructions that have historically left women, teachers, and those in composition dismissed as laborers, without standing to participate as professionals.

Material Conditions

Perhaps the best recent example of the efforts to alter the material conditions of teaching through an act of scholarly publication is Schell and Stock's *Moving a Mountain*. I admire this book and these two women a great deal. I also share many of their concerns about the excessive use of contingent labor to teach first-year courses, especially in composition. But I am troubled by the repetition of distinctions and the use of language that works against what I take as their motive of altering conditions that devalue teachers and their work with students. In the entire collection of *Moving a Mountain*, there are only three articles that address in any way the intellectual dimensions of teaching as a contingent faculty member. Eva Brumberger's piece, "The Best of Times, The Worst of Times: One Version of the 'Humane' Lectureship," explains the criteria for moving from a probationary to an extended-term academic professional lecturer position (P/ET APL) as including the requirement that such NTT faculty stay current in the field and continue to grow professionally. Barry Maid's essay "Non-Tenure-Track Instructors at UALR [University of Arkansas, Little Rock]: Breaking Rules, Splitting Departments" includes a brief discussion of the money that allowed NTT faculty to attend professional conferences with the result that these individuals began to submit panel proposals and write professional articles even though they were not required to do so. Although Maid does not spell out the consequences of these behaviors, it is easy to see that once NTT faculty are "publishing," a number of questions are likely to arise. For example, if *some* NTT faculty members can manage to publish, should *all* such faculty members be expected to do so? If the expectations for these faculty members become so like the expectations for TT faculty as to be indistinguishable, what is the rationale for the lower pay, status, and benefits associated with their rank? If the distinction is built around the interest in classroom practices, students, or pedagogy, what happens to TT faculty members who have centered their careers on the same set of interests?

Only the concluding essay "The Scholarship of Teaching: Contributions from Contingent Faculty," written by Patricia Stock, Amanda Brown, David Franke, and John Starkweather, develops in a substantive way the intellectual issues that classroom teachers, TT or not, can open up for investigation and consideration through the production of teaching portfolios, reflective journals, or conversations centered on evaluating the intellectual engagement of teachers in their practice of teaching.

I do not mean to suggest by this observation that *Moving a Mountain* is not an important contribution to the field of composition studies, indeed, to all of higher education's consideration of the material conditions of teaching and the exploitation of contingent faculty. But I do find it significant that the volume concentrates its focus and its rhetoric with the language of labor and not the language of profession or scholarly knowledge. Much like Haley's separation of classroom teachers from principals, superintendents, and university presidents, the separation of contingent teachers of composition from other teacher-scholars in higher education seems to me a grave misstep. Of course, these teachers are right to be concerned about the material conditions of their work, but casting those concerns as issues of labor and not as issues of our profession reinscribes teaching as labor and professors as professionals because of their scholarly expertise alone. Ignoring the intellectual features of teaching, especially the teaching of contingent faculty, cedes a ground many of us in composition do not wish to relinquish so easily: teaching *can* be a site of intellectual work and ought to be evaluated in those terms regardless of one's rank within the bureaucracy.

Evaluating teaching in the same ways that we evaluate scholarship—setting up criteria of excellence, or teaching awards, creating reports of classroom practices or measuring outcomes either through student success or satisfaction—is, of course, better than ignoring teaching altogether; it is not the same, though, as considering whether the teaching that is being done is a part of an intellectual project, involves students or the teacher in an intellectual activity, or is informed by scholarly expertise or systematic study. In other words, evaluating teaching by a systematic standard can be just as artificial as measuring scholarship by counting pages produced without noticing whether many of those pages say the same things to the same audience or develop different aspects of an intellectual project. Either might be very good work, necessary and, appropriate, but good work is not necessarily the same as work that pushes knowledge forward, applies knowledge in new ways, extends knowledge into new areas, or connects knowledge from different fields. As we saw in the historical constructions of how teachers should be prepared for the classroom, teaching can be either a simplistic transference of knowledge or a complex relationship informed by disciplinary expertise, careful analysis of the lived experience of classroom interactions, and intentional interventions in the learning processes of others.

Therefore, much of what passes as efforts to recognize teaching actually serves to reinforce the prejudices that teaching is performance and not intellectual activity, that scholarship is superior because it *automatically* requires more education, intellect, and effort than does teaching. If we stop to consider our own experiences as students, teachers, and colleagues more closely, however, we will recognize how illogical this set of assumptions really is. We have all known (or been) really talented teachers. They may have been individuals who cared deeply about their students, or ones who knew the content material of their course thoroughly; they may have used innovative techniques to make their classes lively and interesting or simply insisted that students learn the material and then set about making sure they did so. Good teachers are not always good for the same reasons, any more than good writing always has the same explicit features.

While it may be appropriate to have teachers who care deeply about their students and relate to them on a personal level, inspiring them to love learning or motivating them to further study, when teaching is limited to such romanticized relationships, it echoes the earlier view of teaching as "mothering," merely the natural nurturing work of women with little intellectual dimension. Teachers who construct their own identity around such a vision, whether male or female, frequently have no theory of instruction when the personal relationship fails or when their own personal lives demand more of their energy. It is from such limited constructions of teaching that institutions can justify hiring individuals with little disciplinary expertise to occupy first-year courses.

Likewise, we have all known (or been) teachers who go through the motions, perhaps even with satisfactory results, but our engagement in the course (or that of our students) could only be said to be robotic. When teaching is defined as the transference of knowledge or skill, there is little reason to stay engaged once the material is known. For students this means the metaphors of "jumping through hoops," "getting done," "doing enough to get by" that suffice as learning. For teachers, such a construction makes it essential that different courses be taught in order to provide variety and excitement to the otherwise dull routine of teaching. Think of how we list courses and scholarship on our curricula vitae, for example; every article, every conference paper, is listed and considered positive evidence of our intellectual productivity. Courses taught, however, are listed only by name, appearing once no matter how many different versions of the course we have offered.

We have also all known (and unfortunately probably also have been) bad teachers, and bad teachers are bad for equally diverse reasons. But, can we recognize as students, colleagues, or teachers the way that classroom activities are informed by intellectual background or contemplation? Can we separate the informative and successful course from one that articulates a new relationship between learners and knowledge? Do we reward creativity, invention, experimentation, and long-term growth in teaching the way we do in scholarship?

Scholars like Evan Watkins and Bruce Horner have argued that all of the work going on in higher education is intellectual *work*—we are all laborers—and they are right, of course, from the perspective of the commodification of higher education (Watkins; Horner "Traditions"). Horner does an especially thorough job of laying out the ways that teaching and composition have been constructed as belonging to the collective enterprise of institutions while scholarship is said to be the product of the individual. These constructions allow scholarly publications to be commodities that adhere to the individual. Teaching (even the creation of new courses) or service (even complex administrative innovations) are constructed as merely skilled labor, unable to travel with the individual to a new location and therefore unable to increase the value of the individual in the economic system of higher education. But Horner's analysis demonstrates that both scholarship and teaching are dependent on the material conditions that support and enable these different productions. Horner's argument is that denying the underlying material conditions that support scholarship, and ignoring the intellectuality embedded in all labor, creates the distinctions that pit classroom teaching against scholarship or contingent faculty against tenured faculty. I would add that because teaching has historically been associated with the less educated, less worthy female, and because composition classrooms are the site where the newest levels of literacy meet the newest levels of common schooling, it is all the more important to resist dichotomies and discourse patterns we know have been historically unsuccessful. And one of the most unsuccessful to date—at least in terms of gaining the status, independence, and the control associated with professionals—has been the turn to the language of labor to argue for better material conditions for teaching.

5 / Standing to Speak

In the last chapter, I suggested that our current discussions of the problems in higher education, particularly the problems so prevalent in composition programs, are hampered by dichotomies that keep scholarly expertise and professionalism separate from the material conditions of teaching within a bureaucratic institution. Such dichotomies, and the inherited and unexamined language that construct them, keep us from imagining productive alternatives to current structures. Examining this inherited language can interrupt the cycle, providing a foothold from which to evaluate and choose the practices we wish to continue and those we want to abandon.

Pitting scholarship against teaching, for example—which happens regularly within routines such as preparing graduate students, awarding tenure or promotion, or hiring contingent faculty—is underwritten by a long history that equates teaching with "women's work," empty of intellectual activity. These practices, and the dichotomy they construct of scholarship and teaching, simultaneously reinscribe the cultural constructions that most people in the current world of American academics reject when confronted with them more explicitly. In other words, most academics do not believe that women are incapable of intellectual activity, unsuited for public roles, or in need of supervision and direction from male superiors. Even the most conservative academics would be embarrassed to be caught behaving as if they did believe in these nineteenth-century constructions of women. It is not at all uncommon, however, to find those who will insist that teaching is a simple activity, devoid of much intellectual interest, merely the job to be done in the bureaucracy that is higher education, even though such a construction is just as thoroughly inherited from an earlier time and just as irrational as the old beliefs about women. Most will not admit to such beliefs when they are put so bluntly, of course, but a number of their actions and assumptions make those prejudices against teaching more than clear to anyone who looks carefully. Unfortunately, the practices that devalue teaching are even more common than those that discriminate against women, and there are no legal prohibitions to leverage in the effort to get teaching to be recognized as intellectual work.

Likewise, the dichotomy of profession versus labor relies on a set of class and gender distinctions that infected education in the nineteenth century, equating scholarship with professionals and teaching with labor in the process. Explicit concern for the material conditions of work was excluded from the domain of professional organizations, except occasionally in the form of altruistic concern for the labor of subordinates. Thus, teachers—whether disenfranchised elementary teachers of the nineteenth century or contingent composition faculty of the late twentieth century—are left with the language of labor, language that further positions them as nonprofessionals.

The reductive constructions of teaching as a simplistic transference of knowledge or skill or as attention to the learner via nurturing and an ethic of care natural to women and akin to mothering ignore the intellectual activity that is implied in the newest definitions of literacy. Courses of teacher preparation that focus on new teachers merely needing to become comfortable with a new role or a set of authoritative and bureaucratic functions further empty teaching of intellectual activity, position it as "women's work," and attach it to the world of labor rather than profession. These dichotomies are so much a part of our lived experience that we do not consider it possible to change them even if we notice their existence. Even I would not argue that we can ignore or erase the distinctions between scholarship and teaching, professionalism and bureaucratic labor, but these terms need not be perceived as oppositional, and our practices can be altered to require both/and rather than either/or.

In fact, in many ways, institutions of higher education already require both scholarship and teaching, both professional expertise and obedience to systemic boundaries. Likewise, teaching is more properly understood to be the complex interactions of teacher, student(s), and content rather than any one of these to the exclusion of the rest. Teachers cannot be prepared to make decisions as professionals without a rich preparation in theories of knowledge and learning, careful study of content material, and practice in reflective interventions in the processes of learning that acknowledge the entirety of the cultural construction that is education. Altering the practices that perpetuate unreasonable and outdated balances of power ought to be possible if we attend to the language that justifies and constructs those cultural practices and hold ourselves and others accountable for the ideals we profess.

What follows in this chapter are some examples of such efforts to alter these balances of power and insist instead on both/and constructions of our academic lives as well as on this more complex understanding of teaching. Since each of us is embedded in the specifics of our own locations, I do not mean to suggest that there are easy or universal solutions to the complex problems of our professional lives. Nor do I mean to suggest that solutions to material conditions like course loads, tenure processes, or the use of contingent faculty (even if such solutions could be managed) would automatically alter the discursive constructions that underwrite the identity of university professors, institutions of higher education, or the role of education in a democracy. It is difficult to talk about cultural constructions like identity or education, though, without talking about concrete practices and every concrete practice is located in a material world. Even when an apparently successful response to a local situation has been arranged, the context and the solution must be evaluated and continually revised, and it is unlikely that the local solution can be imposed wholesale elsewhere.

The hardest work of this project has been to move into the current times, to the discussions and criticism of higher education and literacy instruction that are the current location for concerns about common schooling for the democracy, and not slip into considering only material conditions. This project, remember, is interested in language, history, *and* practice. There are principles that we can learn from the study of the past and from the close attention to the discourse that surrounds us that can help us reconsider various practices. And, reconsidering practices in relation to the discursive patterns we have learned to recognize may provide alternative responses to reform. The effort in this final chapter, then, is to invite readers to consider a question that arises from the analysis of the prior chapters: what reforms might those of us in composition undertake to interrupt the historical patterns that constitute teaching as merely "women's work," unimportant, and anti-intellectual?

Eileen Schell does a thoughtful job of summarizing into four categories the various reforms addressing contingent faculty in composition in her book *Gypsy Academic and Mother-Teachers*. Reformers have, Schell argues, addressed these problems by suggesting

- the elimination of composition as a requirement, thereby reducing the need to staff so many courses or hire so many teachers;
- the conversion of part-time positions into tenure-track positions with lower enrollment caps per course and a lighter teaching load, thereby ensuring more equitable working conditions and a better job market for new graduates of Ph.D. programs;
- the creation of more professional contingent faculty positions without the expectation for research, thereby providing more job security based on merit but formalizing the two-tier system that already separates contingent teachers from tenured faculty scholars; or
- the formation of unions and coalitions in higher education to collectively achieve better working conditions for the majority of university faculty and employees. (90–102)

From Schell's point of view, each of these positions has potential, but only the unionizing/collectivist solution takes into account the "larger issues confronting higher education; attacks on tenure and on politicized teaching, cuts to public educational funding, increased teaching loads, and broader attempts to redefine and restructure faculty careers" (118). Schell notes the reluctance among many tenured faculty toward changes that reposition teaching and service but urges that they recognize how their own well-being is threatened by the growing reliance on contingent teachers. So, she calls for educating graduate students about material conditions of higher education and the realities of the academic lives they are likely to encounter and urges professional organizations and their members to work collectively to uncover facts and insist on better working conditions (117–20).

While we may agree with Schell about the need to be honest with graduate students about the perils of academic life and the realities of the job market, few who are already enrolled in graduate study seem to be much deterred by such information. Perhaps it is human nature to believe that each one of us will be the exception to the rule; perhaps it is a deep and abiding belief in meritocracy. Schell's call for collective action through professional organizations is also reasonable; statements that articulate reasonable, even idealized, professional standards and practices can be very helpful in local situations, precisely because they carry the authority of the profession. But Schell's faith in unionizing and her reliance on the language of labor politics is not likely to get us very much further than it got Margaret Haley's elementary teachers. Conditions may momentarily improve for some classroom teachers, but we will not alter the devalued and feminized constructions of teaching that are at the heart of these conditions by relying on language that also constructs such work as labor rather than as professional and intellectual.

Likewise, Richard Miller concludes his analysis of four attempts to reform education in *As If Learning Mattered: Reforming Higher Education* by arguing for those who would become professors to understand their careers to be that of "intellectual bureaucrats." For Miller, this term signals the recognition that our academic interests are constrained by the material conditions of limited funds and competing interests, as in any other bureaucracy. Those in composition, he argues elsewhere, can become adept at reading this bureaucracy and crafting appropriate local responses through our skill in persuasive rhetoric, if we are willing to give up our aspirations to be a discipline, forgo trying to get others in the university to care about teaching, and "embrace the very activity that is so disdained across the disciplines: serving entry-level students" (Miller "A Writing Program's" 247).

As John Brereton's review of *As If Learning Mattered* so rightly points out, Miller—unlike recent critiques of higher education and the state of English departments by Cary Nelson, Michael Bérubé, Alvin Kernan, David Damrosch, Bill Readings, and John Guillory— is at least recognizing that teaching composition is a large part of what English departments do (Brereton 494). Brereton also praises Miller for insisting that English professors be realistic about their aspirations and "find our fulfillment in those narrow parameters [credentialing, policing the bounds of knowledge and passing on information and skills], not in earth-shaking pronouncements about the value of the liberal arts or in revolutionary discourse" (497).

Miller is certainly correct about the futility of trying to change structures without recognizing the interests that keep them in place. Likewise, his observation that academic life is constrained by institutional concerns more indicative of a bureaucracy than of some romanticized vision of an intellectual utopia is incontrovertible. Many of us would agree that there can be considerable pleasure as well as fulfillment in the local efforts of teaching and program development. Miller's many versions of this argument, however, begin by accepting the power imbalance between composition and other areas of English studies as natural and appropriate, a starting point that must negate the rest of his argument. I, for one, do not agree that composition is not a discipline, though I do accept that it is one that in many ways is unlike literature. My interests in teaching, literacy, and students requires every bit as much theory and knowledge as do the interests of my colleagues in literature. I do not believe that my scholarship is any less an act of teaching than my teaching is an act of scholarship.

I happen, like most of the rest of my readers, to earn a salary for working within an institution. Such a position does not make me not a professional any more than the lawyer or doctor who is employed by institutions that specialize in litigation or medicine are somehow transformed into mere workers rather than professional experts because of their employment status or location. How can accepting the language that makes my interests and expertise "service," or that limits instruction in literacy to the "entry-level," adequately represent my work, my knowledge or my *professional* standing? If we are indeed witnessing the dawning of a new form of our profession as Miller claims, how will employing an old, outdated, degrading language help us to craft an appropriate new identity or argue for different arrangements of power? How could accepting such language as this, even using it ourselves, ever possibly appeal to the same people who aspire to be, in Miller's terms, "public intellectuals," let alone encourage them to reimagine teaching and composition as sites for such activities?

Both Schell and Miller agree that higher education is not likely to eliminate the NTT positions on which it has come to rely, especially in the economic hard times that have recently found many universities struggling to meet payroll costs, accommodate increased enrollments, and encourage new areas of study. Contingent faculty are, it seems, going to be with us for a very long time. And contingent faculty are not the only victims of impossible material conditions. Not-yet-tenured TT faculty face increasing pressure to publish multiple scholarly books with university presses or articles in prestigious journals at the same time that funding for library subscriptions and purchases is cutting demand for exactly those publications. Many universities ask assistant professors to teach only slightly less than NTT faculty, participate in departmental and university committees, maintain an active publication record, and to do so without summer funding, contributions to retirement plans, or sabbaticals prior to tenure. Compression of salaries for associate professors is also a material condition of many lives in academia. Merit pay raises being eliminated or capped at ridiculously low levels by state legislators or by the fiscal realities of alumni donations and limited tuition are certainly material conditions that stretch far beyond the ranks of contingent faculty. Awarding merit only for scholarly publication is detrimental to the many tenured faculty who spend their time conferencing with students, developing new courses, or serving on committees. These conditions may well stay with us for some time as well, and they seem just as detrimental to the overall well-being of higher education as the use of contingent faculty.

Both Miller and Brereton are right to be more than a bit exasperated at the moral outrage of well-established professors like Cary Nelson who do not even bother to hide their denigration of composition. But if we are going to act locally, as Miller and Schell would have it, how will we judge which of the many local actions to take? What tools will we bring to bear to understand these competing interests? What arguments will we employ to forge coalitions with others, including those others who would be constructed as "management" in the language of labor?

What is missing in these critiques, I would argue, is attention to the language that has constructed these very conditions, language that has repeatedly positioned composition, teaching, and women as inferior, nonintellectual, and "naturally" concerned with mere service. James Boyd White has demonstrated repeatedly in his work with legal discourse that it is the attention to language and rhetorical patterns that can provide a means to judge, including, I would argue, judging which of those small local actions we should take and which we should redirect (see especially *Justice as Translation*). Refusing to surrender the ground of professional legitimacy seems to be an essential component of maintaining a position from and a language with which to judge and act.

What would it mean, then, to use the position and language of profession to respond to reform? How would we revise our inherited language to better represent the both/and of our lived experience instead of the either/or dichotomies that so devalue and misrepresent those of us who teach literacy? This is exactly the question I have struggled with throughout this project, indeed, throughout my entire academic career. I will not pretend, as said earlier, to have the answers to these complicated problems that have vexed so many others. What I can do, though, is suggest five areas for further collective consideration: choice, difference, hierarchies, preparation, and professing.

Allowing for Choice

Cheryl Glenn's recent arguments about the uses of silence are a generative analogy for considering the different possibilities open to literacy teachers. Glenn's careful study of silence in the cases of Anita Hill's testimony in the Clarence Thomas hearings and in Lani Guinier's nomination as attorney general provides a useful corrective to the assumption that silence is always powerless and feminine. As Glenn demonstrates, Hill "held power of the men who didn't know what she knew, let alone what she might say. When she refused to testify, she held power for the same reasons. But as soon as she spoke, the white male senators sat silently judging her to be a liar" (5). Likewise, when the White House prohibited Guinier from explaining her writings on affirmative action, she was rendered powerless while Bill Clinton's silence in the same situation was a powerful act of refusal to support. For Glenn, these different uses of silence are rhetorically different depending on whether they were chosen or imposed. Because composition and teaching have also been constructed as feminine and powerless, it is easy to think that such a construction is a "natural," inevitable state of affairs. But what if we *choose* these areas for our life's work?

Unlike the stories many in our field tell, I did not aspire to be something other than a teacher. I think I always wanted to teach because school encouraged me to ask questions and rewarded me for doing so. The literacy practices and attitudes toward education that I grew up with were very much like those described in Shirley Brice Heath's depiction of southern, working-class families in her ethnographic study *Ways with Words*. Indeed, my father left the paper mills that coexist with the cotton mills in Heath's Roadville to wire houses with electricity and eventually raised us into the middle class with a contracting business. But economic success did not mean the attitudes about learning, children, women, or literacy had changed. Though I did not know the history, and was unaware of class differences in my mostly white childhood, I saw school just as those many nineteenth-century working-class and immigrant women did: as a way out and up.

So, I always wanted to teach, even though I was not always the best student and certainly did not have access to a privileged education. I got better at learning mostly because of my teachers and because I was good at talking my way into meaning and understanding. I expected to teach in the public schools and as an undergraduate prepared to teach the full range of "language arts" with a major in speech communication and minors in theater and English. Exempted from the first term of required composition on the basis of SAT scores, I was bewildered by the routine of the second course. Although we surely did something more, what I remember of that class is that on Mondays and Wednesdays we studied syllogisms, and on Fridays we wrote an essay in response to a topic or question scribbled on the blackboard. On Mondays, after returning our themes—graded but without comments—the teacher, a senior member of the English department, continued the lessons on syllogisms. I suppose our papers showed we lacked logic, but the connections between those practice exercises, the essays we wrote, or the grades we earned were never clear. I had no other instruction in writing in college, let alone in the teaching of writing, though I was clearly preparing for a teaching career. I did have one literature professor who asked me my junior year how I could be "so smart in class and so stupid on paper." When I went to her for help, worried that I would not be able to teach writing since I apparently could not write well myself, she pointed to the missing comma before a "but" on a recent in-class essay exam and told me that "but always has a comma in front." I took an independent study my last term with another professor and encountered revision for the first time. That was 1975.

My first paid teaching assignment came the following year when I entered the Peace Corps. I taught 120 female students with twenty books of each title required for the British exams in literature and language. Few of my students would advance from the ordinary level (our equivalent of high school) to the advanced level (the equivalent of our junior colleges) or from the advanced level to university. These students were not incapable; they had simply been born in a country that could not afford to offer enough seats for all who wanted an education. Their limited chances for advancement did not keep my students from studying hard, for all of these young girls were ensured of a more secure economic future just by attending high school, "sitting the exam," and thereby increasing their bride price.

I learned about teaching writing in this rural Kenyan setting when my efforts to have students diagram sentences produced perfect sentence parsing and no improvement in the compositions they wrote. I began to read the few books on teaching left behind by an earlier volunteer and discovered that ESL teachers already knew that grammar instruction would not improve speaking or writing ability. When I returned to the states and earned a master's degree in English education, I had my first composition pedagogy course. Though I was not a teaching assistant, I did find a contingent teaching position at a language institute, teaching intensive English (both academic and conversational) to foreign adults who had already been admitted into graduate programs in the States. I still planned to teach high school, but when my husband took a position as an attorney in rural Texas working as an advocate for migrant farmworkers, local politics had me blacklisted before I could make it from one school to the next. The university thirty miles away was more liberal and willing to hire me as an adjunct.

I taught a number of different courses as an adjunct—a reading skills class, special courses for the few international students, an ESL methods course for local teachers, and eventually first-year composition. The local schools were offering starting salaries for new teachers with a bachelor's degree that were close to double what I was making as an adjunct, but I was intrigued by the work I was doing in this regional university. I was learning a great deal about writing instruction, mostly from reading in the field, but also because I had TT colleagues who were willing to spend time talking with me about what I was seeing in my classes and in my students' papers. I even had the opportunity to participate in committee work, to sit in on others' classes, to begin to attend professional conferences. When I served on an English department textbook-selection committee and then attended the department meeting at which the chair of the program recommended a book the committee had rejected, I began to feel that my individual efforts were simply not sufficient. When I watched an undergraduate writing award go to a student who had produced the precise formula dictated by her instructor and had the program chair patronizingly pat me on the shoulder when I objected that the process was not fair to the other students who produced more thoughtful and original work, I decided I would apply to doctorate programs. My decision was pragmatic; I recognized that I needed the credentials of those letters after my name in order to have standing to speak in any department where I might work. My decision was also one of desire for knowledge; learning from one class at a time, reading on my own, and talking to only a few other colleagues was a slow way to build up the expertise I needed to be effective in either the classroom or department debates. I remember that the acceptance letter I received awarding me a teaching assistantship included a paragraph about the falling job market and the difficulties of earning a TT job; I do not remember giving such information more than a moment's thought. That was 1987.

I do not know that my story is either typical or all that unusual. I had desires and interests and aspirations, and all were altered by the circumstances of my life. I made choices based on my best thinking at the moment about the options available to me. I was lucky to have the support of my family and to only rarely encounter prejudices that kept me from achieving my goals. Many people in composition tell stories like mine, stories that demonstrate agency and choice rather than imposed silence or exploitation. Those of us who *choose* to center our careers on literacy and teaching seem to be in a very different position from those who have such work thrust upon them or believe that it is the compromise they have been forced to make. Indeed, to prepare oneself for such a career through advanced study, to understand the classroom as a site for knowledge making rather than for knowledge transmission, enables teachers to claim *professional* status that is simply not available to those who see teaching as contract labor.

Many of the NTT faculty that I work with also have chosen their contingent employment from among other options available to them. Some of them have side careers as professional writers but enjoy the interactions with students. One or two are making a transition from teaching high school. Several of them are in positions much as I was as an adjunct: raising a family and so wanting a more flexible schedule than most full-time jobs, even teaching jobs in public schools, provide; tied at least temporarily to a particular locality where employment options are limited; just beginning careers and wanting more experience before deciding on advanced education. Obviously, some of them are frustrated with their lack of success on the academic job market, but most are actively crafting the curricula vitae they need to try again, and more than a few have met with success after a year or two as full-time lecturers. Several are doctoral students who have run out of funding or, more commonly, have lost the sense of direction that will enable them to finish the dissertation; they need the time, money, and resources of a university that full-time employment will give them while they figure out their next options. At least one has left higher education to teach in the public schools at a much higher salary and with a shorter commute. I do not mean to suggest that the conditions of contingent faculty are not, therefore, worth improving, but I would argue that it is demeaning to see these colleagues only as the downtrodden and abused and not as active participants in their own lives. All of us are both victims of our circumstances and capable of agency.

Choosing the terms of one's own identity does not, of course, eliminate the gender and class biases placed on us by institutional structures or by the discursive constructions of others. Glenn's description of Hill being judged by the male senators she confronted or the power imbalance of Guinier as nominee versus Clinton as president make it clear that gender is still very much a force in the constructions of power that surround us. Likewise, the statistical evidence recounted in chapter 4 about the disproportionate effect of job market cuts on women or the skewed numbers in the tenure ranks within composition make it hard to deny that women are disadvantaged just by being women. Still, *choosing* the terms of our identity does provide a ground on which to stand while professing our existence and insisting on appropriate recognition. Because composition draws on so many different disciplinary perspectives, it is possible to find a number of very different life stories behind the individuals who occupy the field. Some come from literary study or classical rhetoric programs. Others emerge from schools of education, linguistics, reading, English as a second language, business or technical backgrounds, journalism, or creative writing. Because all these disciplines can be informative to our work with literacy and teaching, most in the field recognize the value of interdisciplinary collaborations. Indeed, the value of collaboration can help us reimagine the construction of a first-year course as something other than bureaucratic concern for consistency or Foucauldian panopticism that keeps individuals from exercising academic freedom. I have more to say about such collaboration on shared work in the later section of this chapter, but I first want to continue considering the implications of belonging to a field that draws on so many different perspectives and that includes people from such diverse routes of preparation.

Accommodating Difference

If the study of literature was a prime example of the nineteenth century's attempts to organize knowledge, the rise of composition programs, with their interest in literacy, is surely a confirmation of the postmodern view of knowledge as contingent, overlapping, and culturally constructed. Instead of separating knowledge into discrete units and departments, the current trend to see knowledge as interconnected and mutually informing suggests that individual departments vying for pieces of an ever shrinking budget is an outdated structure at best. Composition programs are thus already positioned to help institutions imagine more creative structures. Some composition programs, most famously the one at the University of Syracuse, have seceded from English to form their own departments.

While such separation may be appropriate in those local situations, composition's long ties to an enlarged view of English studies makes it difficult to argue for secession as a solution for most programs.

Indeed, rather than continuing the nineteenth-century structure of individual departments, composition would be wiser to argue for an alternative structure in keeping with its interdisciplinary perspectives. Centers for writing studies, like the ones at the University of Illinois–Urbana and Duke University, for example, provide an institutional site different from departments but more in keeping with the multiplicity that informs our field. These nondepartmental structures have their own set of problems and can still be caught in institutional politics, but their presence creates an alternative to the competition and separation inherent in splitting composition from English. Whether the formal structure of our institutions recognizes the interdisciplinary perspective of composition, our field cannot escape the way literacy and teaching draws from and contributes to a wide range of scholarly connections that are far too numerous to list. It is precisely this richness of connections that makes those in composition more open to collaborations; we recognize the impossibility of knowing all that might be relevant to our interests and have learned from our work with students the benefits of shared knowledge making.

Given this reality, however, those in composition have a responsibility to ensure that the local practices of our own institutions recognize the range of legitimate scholarship and preparation within our field. For example, in hiring committees, we might have to explain that someone with degrees in education or communication can be just as qualified for a given position as someone with a more traditional English degree profile. We may also have to insist that scholarship in composition does not always focus on textual analysis. Similarly, at tenure and promotion considerations, senior faculty have to be prepared to explain how an individual's career profile reflects academic values and to insist on the full range of a teacher-scholar's work being included in external reviews. We may also argue for qualified candidates from the contingent faculty ranks to be considered for promotion into TT positions.

Our professional organizations have already begun taking steps to articulate standards that help support arguments for fair assessments of the full range of faculty work. The two best examples are the MLA's Commission on Professional Service, which was discussed briefly in the last chapter, and the Writing Program Administrators' (WPA) document on evaluating program directors. Remember that I criticized the MLA Commission for reinscribing the distinction between scholarship and teaching, but their efforts were headed in the right direction. If instead of naming scholarship, teaching, and service as the sites for faculty work, the commission had named actual sites—classrooms, publications, committees, community organizations, tutoring conferences—its matrix would neither have perpetuated the automatic dichotomy between teaching and scholarship nor denied the intellectual dimensions of any of these sites. Such a small revision would recognize that teaching occurs both inside and outside formal classrooms and that creating knowledge can happen within publications or classrooms.

Likewise, the WPA document, though focused on evaluating the intellectual dimensions of program directors, provides a framework for evaluating faculty activities by defining "intellectual work" on the basis of four criteria:

- it generates, clarifies, connects, reinterprets, or applies knowledge based on research, theory, and sound pedagogical practice;
- it requires disciplinary knowledge available only to an expert trained in or conversant with a particular field;
- it requires highly developed analytical or problem solving skills derived from specific expertise, training, or research derived from scholarly knowledge; and
- it results in products or activities that can be evaluated by peers. (Council of Writing Program Administrators 19–20)

This list, which is much more specific than the MLA commission's categories of intellectual work and academic citizenship, helps individuals, departments, or institutions articulate more precisely what might be expected in merit reviews. The WPA document argues that individual institutions or programs should work collectively to define and then invite evidence of other academic values. Those listed by the WPA, though, certainly seem a good start: innovation, revision, dissemination, rigor, originality, and consistency.

If all faculty work were evaluated with such criteria, scholarship would not be eliminated, but the balance of power would certainly be altered. I am not suggesting that such a change can be unilaterally enacted; nor am I naive about the numerous forces that keep such articulations of faculty work off the table, especially since insisting on multiple sites for demonstrated innovation, revision, and the rest could put those currently in power at a decided disadvantage. I have found the WPA document extremely helpful, however, in suggesting how my own work might be considered, and I believe it serves individuals and the collective that is our field well if we continue to produce such articulations of alternative standards of evaluation.

Indeed, as the director of a university writing center, I worked with other members of the center to identify qualities we could agree were exemplary of good tutoring. While our initial attempts listed many superficial behaviors like arriving on time, finishing appointments in the allotted time, and keeping records accurately, it was not long before we began to articulate other more complicated features of the work of tutoring, including expanding one's knowledge in areas that might inform practice, recognizing alternative methods and experimenting to incorporate them into one's own practice, and helping others learn to tutor. Separating the features we identified into minimum *job* performance and signs of *professional* commitment to the writing center would have given us the ability to describe the differences between beginning and master tutors, to suggest criteria for reappointment, or to argue for institutional distinctions in pay and responsibility. We might also have used our definitions to structure workshops for own faculty, orientation sessions for beginning tutors, or components of graduate student preparation that could have been woven into the department's required teaching seminars. Unfortunately, the initial work was abandoned when the department made the decision to replace the TT faculty director with an adjunct lecturer on a year-to-year contract. The signal that minimum job performance was all that was necessary was clear to everyone, and efforts to articulate professional expectations were forsaken.

Likewise, individuals may find it possible to alter required bureaucratic forms to incorporate alternative versions of recognition for faculty work. My current institution, for example, requires an annual activity report that asks for classes taught, publications and conference presentations, work with graduate students, and professional or institutional service on a standardized form. Since so much of what I do as a program administrator would fall under institutional service without acknowledging the ways this work is similar to teaching or mentoring graduate students, my chair encouraged me to revise the document to better represent my work. Although it takes considerable time for me to do so each year, I find the practice useful both as a way of letting upper administrators know about my activities and as a means of self-assessment. Even without the requirement for such a rigid form, creating a document that categorizes and accounts for how time is spent could help an individual faculty member make decisions about future activities. Collecting such data across programs or departments may provide concrete evidence necessary to argue for institutional support for particular activities or better represent the collective work of faculty to the public.

Recognizing our interdisciplinary perspectives also gives composition programs the unique opportunity of employing graduate students or postdocs from different disciplines. The University of Iowa's Rhetoric Department, which is responsible for that institution's required composition courses, recruits, trains, and then employs graduate students from across the university. Having TA lines to offer talented and interested graduate students in history, anthropology, education, or literature not only gives the program at Iowa visible cultural capital within the institution as departments vie to offer their most promising graduate students this external funding source, but it also brings together instructors with very different backgrounds to work together to teach appropriate academic literacy.

Likewise, the Center for Writing and Teaching at Duke offers postdoctoral positions to graduates of different disciplines, pairing them with talented scholars in their disciplinary departments and offering them the opportunity to enhance their teaching abilities by constructing first-year and advanced writing courses.

While such arrangements cannot work at every institution—many departments do not have enough graduate students to staff their own introductory courses and teaching assistantships usually cost more than the salaries of contingent faculty—composition programs can use such examples to create viable alternatives at their own locales. There is also the danger that arrangements like those at Iowa or Duke can perpetuate the language of teaching as labor, separate from the intellectual work of scholarship; even an arrangement that intends to disrupt this oppositional pattern can end up reinscribing it, as the analysis of the documents in the previous chapters certainly made clear. Thus, how these arrangements are described, justified, and otherwise rhetorically constructed makes a very big difference in whether they are successful in altering the cultural conceptions to which they contribute. Still, many institutions genuinely want to address the problems of writing instruction and to be able to point to concrete efforts they are taking to improve undergraduate instruction. Offering the opportunity for graduate students from numerous disciplines to learn to teach writing-intensive courses in their own disciplines by working within a composition program could be exactly the innovation an institution is seeking.

Such an arrangement, of course, does not mean that composition has no content of its own. Indeed, cross-disciplinary teaching of writing can only be successful when there is a recognition of the expertise required to teach writing rather than merely assign it, and when program faculty are willing to work collaboratively on their shared interests. Faced with the alternative of being able to recruit and hire interested graduate students from any department for a program or turning over first-year writing courses to tenured faculty to conduct as disciplinary seminars, the question of which to choose ought to involve a close consideration of the preparation these teachers will be given to *teach* writing. Evaluating such a decision would depend, of course, on how those different faculty members—whether graduate student or tenured professor—would be encouraged to see their teaching as a site for writing instruction. Would they be open to learning the knowledge necessary to make professional decisions within their classes and not simply assume that their own success as writers (or as teachers of other disciplinary knowledge) had made them competent to teach writing? How willing would they be to define the boundaries of the course collectively?

Disrupting Hierarchies

When teachers in a composition program are invited to articulate the curricular objectives that they will all then follow, they are working together in a way that allows everyone to draw on their own areas of expertise, and they are simultaneously developing a language that forges a common vision. I do not mean this to sound either mysterious or romantically naive; such document production is hard work and can be fraught with the difficulties of personality and departmental politics. But talking together about what a particular course should be, or could be, how it prepares students for subsequent courses, what its common materials and practices might be, and what standards of evaluation should be used to gauge student success provides a shared intellectual task to which every teacher in a program can contribute, whether they are already certified as experts or not. Talking together about such shared interests forces teachers to articulate their practices, examine the assumptions that inform their work, and seek out scholarship that confirms or provides alternatives to their current practices and beliefs. Entered into as an opportunity for one's own continued professional development, collaboration with others on shared tasks can do what single seminars or required workshops can never hope to accomplish: disrupt the hierarchy that treats teaching as nonintellectual labor.

Of course, processes like curriculum design are never really completed; curriculum is always "in progress," and that is just as it should be if individual faculty members are going to be effective in an institutional setting. Sustaining talk about the same curriculum repeatedly, though, is impossible; those who participate year after year can find the repetition of old arguments or the constant need to expose new colleagues to the newest theory that challenges outdated assumptions more than a little tedious. Most programs do not offer a single course, however, and considering each course in a program systematically and carefully can take several years. Moreover, curriculum design is not the only shared task teachers of a common course can undertake; evaluation standards, textbook options, inclusion of media or computer technology, material design, placement of students, connections to public schools through writing institutions or summer camps, and development of service-learning projects that bring literacy into nonacademic settings are only a few of the collaborative projects that composition faculty can undertake to stretch their own professional knowledge and expertise while addressing teaching concerns.

I am not suggesting, of course, that curricular decisions or program development opportunities be made by simple majority votes with everyone else forced to comply with the will of the majority. But I do not believe that curriculum decisions are rightly made by tenured faculty who do not teach the courses either or that program directors can simply dictate rules or practices for others to enact. Such moves would merely reinscribe a version of the dichotomies of power that I argue are outdated and inappropriate. So rather than construct scholars as more knowing than teachers or teaching as empty of professional expertise, composition teacher-scholars can lead discussions in which curriculum objectives are discussed, studied, written down, problematized, reimagined, and finally enacted in concert with those who enter the individual classrooms. Because this work will have been constructed in collaboration, it can then be reexamined, reconsidered, and expanded as a shared cultural construction rather than as the identity of any individual teacher. Such a practice demonstrates the ways that classrooms and teaching can serve as sites for knowledge making not just knowledge transference.

Actually, such work is appropriate for more than composition faculty; every course serves a particular institutional need and departments that work collectively to outline those functions clearly have the best chance of ensuring that their graduates have had reasonably similar courses regardless of the teacher of their particular section. Consistency like this is not merely a bureaucratic concern, for as we saw earlier, consistency is a *professional* academic value as well. Still, administrators certainly understand the necessity of justifying required courses by insisting that they meet well-accepted norms in the discipline or in academia at large. Thus, administrative support is likely to come to those departments that use their professional expertise to provide clear guidelines for their various classes. That is not to say that every course needs to use an agreed-on syllabus or a set of prescribed readings. Indeed, resisting such a regimented notion of curriculum is exactly what is required of professionals. But it is also not the case that anybody can teach anything they want in any class, even if they are full professors.

So, working collaboratively and respecting the insights of classroom teachers who are critically reflective and who consider their courses sites of intellectual work and knowledge making is something composition programs can certainly do. There are any number of local examples of such collaborative efforts, including portfolio groups, teaching circles, and curriculum and textbook selection committees. Participants in such shared work certainly learn from participating in the task at hand, and the sense of investment that makes meaningful changes is a standard of collaboration.

Collaboration is not, of course, a panacea. Working collaboratively requires a consideration of material conditions and considerable patience. When will faculty members have time to talk together about shared interests? Who is responsible for document production? What happens when groups simply cannot agree? Does such work count in merit evaluations for either NTT or TT faculty? Again, the variations in local conditions have to figure in such efforts, and, at any point, the effort to build a shared vision can undercut respect for individual teachers and their expertise. The alternatives, however, have already proved much worse.

Preparing Professional Teachers

If I am correct that the first-year composition course is the newest site for an expected level of common schooling and thus feels the same demands of expanding numbers and the need for teachers that were visible at the end of the nineteenth century in public school systems, then it seems fairly clear that preparing teachers to fill these jobs as professionals and not merely laborers is an important task of composition programs. There are two different venues within which to prepare teachers: graduate programs that prepare future professors and composition programs that currently employ teachers.

The historical examples I have already put forward reveal that poorly prepared teachers were employed to teach, then prohibited from participating in professional organizations, and finally forced to organize as laborers rather than professionals in order to gain appropriate working conditions. Universities would be well served to avoid this pattern and engage every teacher they hire in professional activities. Let me be clear: I am not arguing, as Bruce Horner does in his "Traditions and Professionalization: Reconceiving Work in Composition," that *professional* is a term of disciplinary expertise constructed through the distance maintained between specialized and lay knowledge. For Horner,

> The discourse of professionalism limits how we think of the work of Composition, defining legitimate work as the acquisition, production, and distribution of print codified knowledge about writing: the production, and reception of (scholarly) texts. In this discourse, the work associated with such activities as teaching is deemed "labor," the implementation of the work of professional knowledge. (Horner 375)

Horner's critique accepts uncritically the definition of professionalism that he himself, in the paragraph preceding this one, has identified as a construction that results in "theory and practice, scholarship and teaching [being] set in opposition." If we refuse to accept this opposition, if we imagine instead something like the model of the MLA commission whereby scholarship and teaching are both sites for intellectual work, then profession (and professional discourse) must likewise be reconceptualized. Horner is right that we can learn from our close connection to public school teachers. What we need to learn, however, is not how they behaved as organized labor to ensure some control over their work and well-being, but rather how they were forced to surrender the term *professional* because of the prohibitions of class and gender that limited their education, denied the importance of their concerns, and left them silenced.

Rather than this oppositional and hierarchical construction of *profession*, we can reclaim the term *professional* as defining one who is prepared to make informed, intelligent judgments appropriate for the given situation. Thus, professionals are those who can be trusted to perform their jobs with more than minimal competencies and to demonstrate intellectual engagement in their work. In other words, we can refuse to separate the material conditions of work from the key features of intellectual engagement and decision making inherent in professionalism. We can insist, in fact, that one cannot *be* a professional without both theory and practice, without both specialized expertise and the ability to relate that knowledge to larger public concerns. Thus, whether composition is a discipline that makes knowledge like other, more traditional disciplines is of little significance; what matters is that those of us in composition draw on a wide range of knowledge, often by synthesizing knowledge that comes from different disciplines, but also by testing it against our lived experience in order to make decisions that are often, but not only, centered around issues of teaching.

Because no one, no matter how experienced or talented, is ever done learning to teach; because teaching is a lived experience involving the changing dynamics of individuals in relationship to one another; because knowledge about language, literacy, inquiry, and meaning making is always growing; composition cannot be reduced to a set of skills, a finite body of knowledge, or a simplistic set of teaching behaviors. Since classes and curricula do not exist outside institutional structures—departments, general requirements, prerequisites, and so on—individual teachers must work within a system, and they must work collectively to establish and revise these systems.

As I suggested in the previous section, talking with colleagues is one of the primary ways of forging connections between individual interests and institutional goals. Opportunities to talk together, to create shared documents (course descriptions, program requirements, or criteria for evaluation, for example) are occasions to teach new and old teachers to reconsider their assumptions, to articulate the theories that inform their choices, to share their expertise with one another, and to refine their ability to "read" the classroom as a site for knowledge making.

Activities that further prepare teachers who are already employed—what is commonly known as professional development—can be as simple as offering funds for such teachers to attend professional conferences or as elaborate as the teaching portfolio practices established at the University of Syracuse (for a discussion of this practice, see Stock et al.). Bringing guest speakers to campus and making it possible for classroom teachers to attend, offering NTT faculty opportunities to gain additional expertise and to demonstrate their intellectual and pedagogical growth, and rewarding such faculty who do demonstrate increased knowledge and expertise are other examples of systematic attention to the professional preparation (and growth) of already employed teachers. But all of these efforts can be undercut by actions that suggest that these teachers do not already have knowledge that is important and worthy.

Let me offer an analogy to our students' writing. Most of us recognize that students come into our classrooms, especially our college classrooms, already knowing many things about literacy practices. They may know things we believe are incorrect, like "I" cannot be used in an academic paper. They may know things that are only partially true, like introductions have to tell readers what you will say and conclusions tell them what you have already said. They may know a number of things that we are inclined to believe irrelevant to our purposes, like how football plays are planned and practiced, or how county extension agents count bugs in fields to recommend fertilizers and chemical sprays. They know things they do not realize they know, like how to read a classmate's paper and respond, how to look at an issue from a different point of view, or how to reread their own writing and consider how it might be changed. There is no denying, however, that they know a great deal, and teachers who do not recognize what students know are not likely to be very successful.

Likewise, all of us know things about teaching and learning, but only some of what we think we know is actually correct or useful in any given situation. As I work with beginning teachers, I am often amazed at the connections they are able to make to prior experiences that do not seem like teaching at first glance. Just as often, I am dismayed at the ideas these beginning teachers (or, for that matter, my senior colleagues or even my nonteaching family and friends) have about teaching that come from their own experiences as students. Because teaching is such a complex, human interaction, preparing teachers seems to me to require attention to a number of different facets including those we saw at work in the descriptions of required teaching seminars in chapter 3:

- the teacher and his/her role in the classroom (the "comfort" issues in the Michigan "Pedagogy" course figure in here, but also performance and authority issues like pacing, structure, clarity, setting the tone, and speaking loudly enough as well as the issues of reflective practice that Gallagher's teaching course included);
- the student (the attention to the learner we saw represented in the historical descriptions of courses to prepare teachers certainly fits in this category, but also such issues as cognitive development, group interactions, learning styles and differences, and recognizing and knowing

our limits in helping students in emotional or mental distress);
- the cultural context (Spellmeyer's concern for the history and institutional position of composition or the early NCTE committee's concern that teachers know about public school curricula are good examples of this dimension); and,
- the subject matter (in the case of composition, language and literacy theories; and research, grammar, and rhetoric as well as pedagogical knowledge like effective responding to student work, prompting revision, peer learning strategies and collaboration, and evaluation and assessment).

Thus, even as NTT faculty and graduate students teaching first-year composition continue to be a necessity at most universities, there is little reason to imagine that treating them as skilled labor and not as colleagues will somehow transform them into professionals. Likewise, acting as if preparation for teaching were ever completed seems to me simply laughable given the dimensions listed previously.

I do not mean to suggest that part-time faculty or beginning graduate students ought to have equal responsibility or authority of full professors. Obviously, many of the NTT faculty employed to teach are not prepared to participate in institutional or programmatic decisions. Some are not even interested in doing so. During my own years as a doctoral student, I was careful about what institutional activities I took on, in part because I already had experience in committee work and curriculum development, but also because my long-term commitment was not to that particular institution. In other words, my professional work at that moment took a different venue. I imagine that there will also be moments in my future career (when on sabbatical, for example), when institutional work will not be as appropriate as it has been for me more recently. Allowing for such differences in individual choice and the fluctuations of career cycles can surely be built into local structures that prepare graduate students and the reforms that redefine the full range of faculty work. Assuming that "junior" faculty members are already experienced teachers is often just as incorrect as assuming that NTT faculty or graduate students have no useful knowledge to contribute to discussions of curricula. The many institutions of higher education that now have some form of "teaching effectiveness centers" for supporting continued professional development in teaching are certainly taking an important first step in the ongoing preparation of professional teachers. In fact, few of us in composition probably realize that professional offices of development (PODs) have existed long enough to have their own publications, conferences, and organizations. The Southern Regional Education Board identified eleven such centers as early as 1976, and ten of those had been in existence since 1971 (Southern Regional Education Board 56). Many institutions use their centers to fund innovative uses of technology; select teaching award recipients; or provide supportive, in-class assessments for beginning teachers that are clearly separated from the evaluative visits by the teacher's departmental colleagues or supervisors. Some centers administer student evaluations of courses, provide workshops, or offer courses for graduate students from departments that do not conduct their own TA preparation. There have also been, though, a number of research projects funded by corporate foundations and federal agencies that have originated in these centers. While I cannot take the time in this project to trace the interactions between such scholarship, these centers, and the reform movements that are now better known (like the Pew project for preparing future faculty or the Boyer report I discussed in chapter 2), even a cursory look at this history makes it clear that the connections are numerous (see, for example, Gaff and Simpson's summary of faculty development).

I am not oblivious to how unsuccessful these centers have been in altering the dichotomies of teaching and scholarship or professional and labor. Indeed, there is much in the language and practices of such institutionalized forms of support for teaching that is problematic, but their very presence is another sign that the institutions that employ us are not completely unconcerned about the quality of teaching or the difficulties inherent in preparing professional teachers.

Modifying graduate programs to include more attention to the preparation of teachers is a more common site for efforts to reform the professional preparation of teachers, but it is also a more difficult reformation. In the first place, graduate programs in English departments that perceive their mission as preparing literary scholars have already separated the activities of faculty into teaching and scholarship, literature and literacy. Altering that mission is, for many such faculty members, a denial of their own expertise and life choices and a capitulation to the forces and whims of the job market. Not only are many of these faculty members themselves not interested in teaching, especially teaching literacy courses like composition, they hope for more for their graduate students and believe that the power relations of higher education that privilege scholarship will not change. Why, then, would they participate in preparing younger scholars—whose interests, they imagine, are more akin to their own—for a life based on classroom teaching? It is just such irreconcilable differences that have severed composition programs from literature departments across the country, often to the detriment of both.

English departments that want to concentrate on literature ought to devise ways of preparing their graduate students to teach literature instead of offering them the mixed messages inherent in assigning them to teach composition but devaluing the experience as disconnected from their interests. They might begin by renaming themselves more appropriately as departments of literature. Such a department might use TAs in their introductory literature survey courses, which is usually a standard requirement in the undergraduate curriculum and thus regularly in demand. The department could then reasonably expect graduate students to enroll in a teaching seminar focused on teaching literature rather than on the teaching of composition. Responding to student writing in such a context might be one part of the preparation course, but such courses need not expect students to receive explicit instruction in writing any more than in other introductory courses like philosophy or history. Instead, the focus would be on the conveying of information, designing a course that meets the introductory/survey expectations, and organizing a progression of activities—lectures, discussions, quizzes and longer exams, projects, writing assignments, Web site materials, and so on—that satisfy those curricular goals.

At the very least, literature and creative writing programs ought to be conscious of the divisions they perpetuate by separating themselves from the preparation of teachers and the teaching of composition. All programs within an English department have a responsibility to work to demonstrate the interconnections among these areas of English studies. In fact, the value of interdisciplinarity would suggest that even doctorate programs in narrow literary fields need to find common cause with the work of composition programs and those who prepare teachers at any level. Those who ignore the ways that departments no longer reflect the organization of knowledge or epistemological understandings in a postmodern world do so at their peril and ours.

When graduate programs in English take their responsibilities to prepare future professors for teaching seriously, they will design a logical sequence of teaching assignments for TAs, with appropriate support at each stage along the way, and recognition of the many differences students bring with them into graduate school. In other words, the same sequence and support mechanisms are not appropriate for every graduate student any more than the same practice exercises produce equally competent undergraduate writers. I do not mean to suggest that teaching first-year students is necessarily easier than teaching advanced students; indeed, teaching first-year students may require more experience and expertise than teaching second-year students who are not also confronting the many personal adjustments to college life. Certainly, teaching writing is not easier than teaching literature, especially for those whose first interest is in literature rather than literacy.

Thus, departments that aim to prepare professional teachers

might assign first-year TAs to a senior faculty member teaching a second- or third-year lecture course, invite the TA to prepare one or more lectures during the term and participate in evaluating the students, lead small discussion sections, or otherwise "begin" to teach. If the senior faculty member assumes, however, that the graduate student will learn to teach either by simply watching the performance of the master or by diving in to sink or swim on his or her own, the alternative structure of preparation will be no better at disrupting the dichotomies (and no better a preparation) than the single seminar approach has been. A department, or even a composition program, that intends to be serious about preparing professional teachers will need as much time for careful thought, research, observation, and analysis of results as would be required by any scholarly project.

Several composition programs use tutoring in a writing center as a part of their preparation program for graduate students, but such a rotation ought to take into consideration the very different skills necessary to work with students one-on-one than those needed to lead a whole class. Likewise, automatic reassignment to the writing center for the graduate student who has difficulty in the classroom is not a useful intervention and is unlikely to produce changes in classroom practices. Writing centers can offer more flexible hours than a course, and the pace of writing center work is, for many people, less stressful. Nevertheless, reassigning a graduate student who is "shy" or "disorganized" in front of a class to work in the writing center is not a reasonable pedagogical plan for helping that teacher become comfortable or competent in the classroom. Likewise, because a tutor shows great patience in working with individual students on their writing, there is no guarantee that the tutor is equally skilled in leading an entire class group to discuss representative pieces of their writing together.

Preparing graduate students to teach, then, is a complicated process, because teaching, if rightly understood, is a complicated process already, and teaching teachers is doubly so. While introductory seminars are an important step, then, they cannot be the only step. Graduate preparation to teach could make use of the standard practices of seminars, qualifying exams, advancing to candidacy, and dissertation defenses. Some of my colleagues, for example, routinely require graduate students to produce a presentation appropriate for an undergraduate course on the material they are studying or to design a curricular unit or other teaching-related document within their literary seminars. Likewise, I have heard colleagues argue that qualifying exams should include a question that specifically asks for the pedagogical application of literary material. Several years ago, the University of Michigan's English and Education program transformed one of its required qualifying exams into the submission and evaluation of a teaching portfolio appropriate to the candidate's own areas of interest and expertise. Such efforts are certainly small and incremental changes, but they signify a genuine attempt to combine rather than continue to distinguish teaching and the usual measures of professional expertise.

Finally, I would suggest that many college professors already recognize that nothing so taught them a particular set of material as the need to teach it to someone else. Such insight could allow us to build teaching opportunities into even undergraduate programs. Indeed, several such initiatives have been under way for some time, often in the form of attempts to improve undergraduate teacher-education programs or to recruit talented undergraduates into teaching. One current example is the Teacher Quality Enhancement grants connected to the Holmes Partnerships and funded by the Department of Education (for detailed information, see Teacher Quality Enhancement Forum; Holmes Partnership). Called the SUCCEED Project at my university, this five-year, multimillion dollar grant has funded a number of projects that connect the School of Education, the College of Arts and Sciences, and the Miami-Dade public schools. One project funded by the grant is a peer-led teaching initiative that began by putting successful biology students back into the required entry-level course as discussion leaders for small peer groups (for additional information about the peer-led teaching initiatives in the sciences, see National Science Foundation's Division of Undergraduate Education). While this intervention in a biology lecture course added problem-solving, discussion-oriented pedagogy into the course for the first time and increased student success in the course dramatically, bringing the model into already small, discussion-oriented classes like composition and introductory literature courses emphasizes the potential for such an intervention to enhance the learning of leaders, show them the intellectual dimensions of teaching, and thereby encourage them to think of teaching as a possible career path. Thus, in our adaptation of the peer-led teaching initiative to the English courses, we have added an undergraduate seminar in literacy as both an ongoing support mechanism for these small-group teachers and a way of insisting that even these undergraduates have the opportunity to talk together and learn more about the interconnected scholarship of literacy and pedagogy. Peer leaders are encouraged to approach their teaching experience as a site for knowledge making by learning to observe carefully and reflect on their experiences in relation to theory.

Composition programs that hire undergraduates as tutors for the writing center make a similar use of the potential power of teaching as a venue for learning. Many of these programs, unfortunately, have simply hired talented students to tutor weaker students without using the teaching act itself as a site of knowledge making. Writing center associations have regularly included undergraduate peer tutors in their conferences, however, encouraging them to make presentations about their work and their own learning. Even if what these undergraduates learn in these limited teaching opportunities seems obvious to those of us with more experience, the power of learning firsthand is well worth the effort to provide such opportunities.

Obviously, not every undergraduate can be a tutor, and not every institution has grant money to develop the kind of large-scale initiative with multiple objectives that the SUCCEED grant invites. Instructors who allow students the option to develop teaching units as a final project for a term, however, are allowing undergraduates to learn from the experience of thinking as a teacher. Likewise, in a grammar course, a requirement that students develop an explanation of a particular grammar or mechanical point as "Dear Grammar Lady" columns positioned students, at least momentarily, as teachers, exposing them in a small way to the difference in knowing and teaching others. There are many classes that could ask students to consider the material in relation to a teaching situation, even if that situation were only the need to inform the public through a speech, editorial, or informative Web site.

Professing

Because efforts to reform teachers and teacher preparation are frequently generated by public criticism of education, it is not surprising that the current wave of attention to undergraduate teaching follows on the heels of public criticism of higher education. Ignoring these public concerns is simply not possible; universities not only rely on public support for funding, they also have a responsibility to the culture that is central to their self-definition. As experts with specific knowledge, as teachers engaged in intellectual work, we are invested with the resources to *profess,* and yet we too seldom do so. Like Anne Gere's argument for the value of attending to nonschooled forms of writing and learning, which arises from her historical studies of how often literacy instruction has gone outside the walls of classrooms, my argument is that historical study demonstrates that the repeated efforts to reform teachers in response to public anxieties about literacy instruction has ignored the ways in which teachers have systematically been denied the education essential for professional status and judgment. Once we begin to provide that education, once we treat teaching as another site for our intellectual work, teaching the public can more easily be seen as a part of the work faculty could and should do.

What do I mean by teaching the public? First, our publications, our scholarship, too often speak only to other experts. We leave the translation of the most important—or more likely, the most controversial—portions of our work to journalists who function within the constraints of short time blocks and even shorter page limits and who have their own agendas inflected by their own set of economic rewards and incentives. Rather than abdicate such public presentations to others, universities and professional organizations need to find ways of encouraging faculty to speak directly to public audiences. Of course, some professional educators already have managed to make such public connections. Too often, though, speaking to a lay audience is considered less scholarly and is therefore dismissed within the structures that evaluate faculty work, or such opportunities are reserved for those who have nothing to lose by going public.

A more likely public site for the work of most of us in composition happens when we participate in state or local initiatives connected to our scholarly expertise. Literacy scholars who help with state-mandated assessment projects, for example, are doing important public work but may find their participation more acceptable, and their work more likely to be recognized as appropriate, if it is categorized as "service" within their academic communities. If these scholars are patient enough, they may be able to turn such public work into an appropriate academic publication, or at least a conference paper, so that they can move it from the category of service into the domain of scholarship. But, the more this work strays from a central scholarly project, the more difficult it is to make the case for its inclusion in a career profile.

One colleague I know centers her work on professional discourses, on the literacy practices that distinguish the worlds of work from the world of academia. She has a number of professional publications, a record of outstanding and innovative teaching, and solid evidence of thoughtful institutional service, but when her son was diagnosed with cancer, she became interested in the ways that writing could help families and cancer patients themselves negotiate the new literacy practices they encountered in hospitals and treatment plans. Her work took a much more public turn as she gained grants for displaying the art and writing of these children, participated in family-advocacy teams with medical professionals, and used her scholarly expertise to examine her own experience and those of others like her. Not surprisingly, these new efforts took considerable time and were not always easily executed, especially since they involved collaborations with other parents who were not academics and whose concerns were not necessarily well satisfied by making their writing publishable. The starts and stops of such public connections to intellectual issues, the way this faculty member's projects were limited to local or state communities rather than suitable for the generalizations expected in a more scholarly (read national) project, made it difficult to translate these efforts into academic terms and led to the advice that she delay coming up for tenure until she could show more traditional publications from this work.

Even within institutional settings, the risks of collaborative work, especially across different disciplines must be acknowledged if faculty are to be expected to participate. A language and literacy committee I served on faced just this problem as it worked to develop a three-year symposium project that would bring together faculty from different colleges within the university to share their scholarship on language and literacy issues, propose new team-taught courses, and devise an undergraduate literacy studies minor. The grant that funded our planning work (the same SUCCEED grant I mentioned previously) could potentially also be used to buy out the time of faculty participants, but if the work they would be doing on the symposium did not result in disciplinary publications, there would be few ways to recognize their intellectual engagement in this interdisciplinary, curricular, and institutional effort. Learning to speak across the divides represented by different departments and schools would be no small undertaking; constructing and then shepherding a new minor into existence would be time consuming and potentially unsuccessful; senior faculty members were already overloaded with administrative work and junior faculty simply could not be asked to participate unless the institution would acknowledge the intellectual dimensions of such work.

Thus, whether we aim to publish our scholarship directly to a public audience or to use our scholarly expertise to participate in public situations, we are not always well prepared to do so and the reward structures of higher education do not encourage such activity. Composition, though, is particularly well suited for making such forays into public venues because its interests in literacy, language, and the cultural structures that support these activities have so many possible public connections. Composition has a great deal to gain by considering how such public work could be represented appropriately within institutional and professional terms and structures.

When academics fail to engage public audiences outside our disciplines, when we ignore the implications of our scholarly work, or when we keep our teaching safely out of sight, we help turn universities into mere bureaucracies that use intellectual labor as a commodity, ceding our professional aspirations as the price for speaking only to ourselves. But because this is the way things usually are in the current world of higher education, does not mean that this is how things ought to remain. For me and many others who know the history of the teachers who came before us, too many years have been spent gaining the standing to speak to not now choose when and how we will do so. For me and many others who have chosen to center our professional lives on composition, too much time has been spent in the presence of practices and language from a time long dead to surrender our options for employing other practices and other language in our response to reform.

Works Cited

Index

Works Cited

Allen, Harold B. "Preparing the Teacher of Composition and Communication—A Report." *College Composition and Communication* 3.2 (May 1952): 3–13.

American Council of Learned Societies. "Anna Callender Brackett." *Dictionary of American Biography*. Ed. Allen Johnson. New York: Scribner's, 1929, 1957. 546–47.

———. "Cyrus Peirce." *Dictionary of American Biography*. Ed. Allen Johnson. New York: Scribner's, 1929, 1957. 403.

———. "James Gordon Carter." *Dictionary of American Biography*. Ed. Allen Johnson. New York: Scribner's, 1929, 1957. 538.

Apple, Michael. "Teaching and 'Women's Work': A Comparative Historical and Ideological Analysis." *Teacher's College Record* 86 (Spring 1985): 455–73.

Badger, Reid. *The Great American Fair: The World's Columbian Exposition and American Culture*. Chicago: Nelson Hall, 1979.

Barnard, Henry. "American Institute of Instruction." *American Journal of Education* 2 (1856): 20–32.

Becker, Howard S. "The Nature of a Profession." *Education for the Professions: The 61st Yearbook of the National Society for the Study of Education, Part II*. Ed. Nelson B. Henry. Chicago: U of Chicago P, 1962. 27–46.

Beecher, Catharine. *Suggestions Respecting Improvements in Education*. Hartford, CT: Hartford, Packard and Butler, 1829.

Bérubé, Michael. "The Blessed of the Earth." *Will Teach for Food: Academic Labor in Crisis*. Ed. Cary Nelson. Minneapolis: U of Minnesota P, 1997. 153–78.

Bledstein, Burton. *The Culture of Professionalism*. New York: Norton, 1976.

Board of Censors. *The Introductory Discourse and the Lectures Delivered before the American Institute of Instruction*. Boston: Carter, Hendee, 1834.

———. *The Lectures Delivered before the American Institute of Instruction, Including the Journal of Proceedings*. Boston: William D. Ticknor, 1840.

———. *The Lectures Delivered before the American Institute of Instruction, Including the Journal of Proceedings*. Boston: Ticknor, Reed, and Fields, 1850.

———. *The Lectures Delivered before the American Institute of Instruction with the Journal of Proceedings*. Boston: Amer. Inst. of Instruction, 1868.

Board of Directors. *The Lectures Delivered before the American Institute of Instruction with the Journal of Proceedings*. Boston: Amer. Inst. of Instruction, 1869.

Works Cited

Boyer Commission on Educating Undergraduates in the Research University. *Reinventing Undergraduate Education: A Blueprint for America's Research Universities.* 22 Apr. 2003. <http://naples.cc.sunysb.edu/Pres/boyer.nsf>.

Boyer, Ernest L. *Scholarship Reconsidered: Priorities of the Professoriate.* Princeton, NJ: Carnegie Foundation for the Advancement of Teaching, 1990.

Brackett, Anna C. "Doctors and Teachers. The Relation of the Medical and Educational Professions." *The Lectures Read before the American Institute of Instruction with the Journal of Proceedings.* Ed. Board of Directors. Boston: Amer. Inst. of Instruction, 1875. 45–62.

Brereton, John C. "Review: As If Learning Mattered: Reforming Higher Education." *CCC* 51.3 (Feb. 2000): 494–97.

———. "Review: Four Careers in English." *College English* 61.1 (Sept. 1998): 71–82.

———, ed. *The Origins of Composition Studies in the American College, 1875–1925: A Documentary History.* Pittsburgh: U of Pittsburgh P, 1995.

Brown, Stuart C., and Rebecca Jackson. "Doctoral Programs in Rhetoric and Composition." *Rhetoric Review* 18.2 (Spring 2000): 244–374.

Brumberger, Eva. "The Best of Times, The Worst of Times: One Version of the 'Humane' Lectureship." Schell and Stock 91–106.

Bureau of Education, Dept. of Interior. State School Systems "Table 7: Number and Sex of Teachers. Proportion of Male Teachers." *Report of the Commissioner of Education for the Year 1893–94* 15 (1896).

Butler, Vera Minnie. *Education as Revealed by New England Newspapers Prior to 1850.* Philadelphia: Majestic, 1935.

Button, H. Warren, and Eugene F. Provenzo Jr. *History of Education and Culture in America.* Englewood Cliffs, NJ: Prentice, 1989.

Calhoun, W. B. "Massachusetts Seminary for Teachers: Report of a Select Committee for the House of Representatives," 1827. *American Journal of Education* 2 (1857): 15357.

Carr-Saunders, A. M., and P. A. Wilson. *The Professions.* Oxford: Clarendon, 1933.

Carter, James. *Essays on Public Education.* 1826. New York: Arno, 1969.

Carter, Susan B., and Mark Prus. "The Labor Market and the American High School Girl, 1890–1928." *Journal of Economic History* 42 (Mar. 1982): 163–71.

Clifford, Geraldine Joncich. "Buch und Lesen: Historical Perspectives on Literacy and Schooling." *Review of Educational Research* 54.4 (1984): 472–500.

Clinton, William. "State of the Union." *New York Times* 28 Jan. 1998, final ed.: A19.

Cohen, Sol. *Challenging Orthodoxies: Toward a New Cultural History of Education.* New York: Lang, 1999.

Committee on the Preparation of College Teachers of English. "Report of the Committee on the Preparation of College Teachers of English." *English Journal* 5.1 (1916): 20–32.

———. "Tentative Propositions with Regard to the Professional Training of College Teachers of English." *English Journal* 7.1 (1918): 62–63.

Council of Writing Program Administrators. "Evaluating the Intellectual Work of Writing Administration." *WPA: Writing Program Administration* 22.1-2 (1998): 85–104. 14 Sept. 2001. <http://www.cas.ilstu.edu/english/hesse/intellec.html>.

Cox, John Harrington. "What Is the Best Preparation for the College Teacher of English? Training for Teaching and Training for Research." *English Journal* 2.4 (1913): 207–14.

Cremin, Lawrence. *American Education: The National Experience, 1783–1876*. New York: Harper, 1980.

Ehrenreich, Barbara, and John Ehrenreich. "The Professional-Managerial Class." *Between Labor and Capital*. Ed. Pat Walker. Boston: South End, 1979.

Elsbree, Willard S. *The American Teacher: Evolution of a Profession in a Democracy*. New York: American, 1939.

Enos, Theresa. *Gender Roles and Faculty Lives in Rhetoric and Composition*. Carbondale: Southern Illinois UP, 1996.

Fish, Stanley. "Anti-Professionalism." *New Literary History* 17 (Aug. 1985): 89–108.

Freidson, Eliot. *Professional Powers: A Study of the Institutionalization of Formal Knowledge*. Chicago: U of Chicago P, 1986.

[Friend of Liberty]. "Importance of Education." *Massachusetts Magazine* June 1789: 381.

Gaff, Jerry G., and Ronald D. Simpson. "Faculty Development in the United States." *Innovative Higher Education* 18.3 (1994): 167–76.

Gallagher, Chris. *Fall 2002 Graduate Course Description Booklet: Engl 957—Comp Theory and Practice*. 24 June 2002. <http://www.unl.edu/english/html/CDgrF02.html>.

Geiger, Roger, ed. *The American College in the Nineteenth Century*. Nashville: Vanderbilt UP, 2000.

Gere, Anne Ruggles. "Kitchen Tables and Rented Rooms: The Extracurriculum of Composition." *CCC* 45.1 (1994): 75–92.

Glenn, Cheryl. "Silence: A Rhetorical Art for Resisting Discipline(s)." *Journal of Advanced Composition* 22.2 (Spring 2002): 261–92.

Green, Steven. Parental Leave Policy Faculty Senate Legislation #2001-27(B). 12 July 2002. <http://www.miami.edu/faculty-senate/2001-27-parentalleave.doc>.

———. "Pursuing a Degree in the Same Department Where an Academic Appointment Is Held." Faculty Senate memo, 7 Aug. 2001.

Greenough, Chester Noyes. "An Experiment in the Training of Teachers of Composition for Work with College Freshmen." *English Journal* 2.2 (1913): 109–15.

Griggs, Irwin. "The Professional Status of the Composition Teacher." *CCC* 3.3 (1952): 10–12.

Haber, Samuel. *The Quest for Authority and Honor in the American Professions, 1750–1900.* Chicago: U of Chicago P, 1991.

Haley, Margaret. *Battleground: The Autobiography of Margaret A. Haley.* Ed. Robert Reid. Urbana: U of Illinois P, 1982.

———. "Why Teachers Should Organize." *Journal of Proceedings and Addresses of the National Educational Association of the United States* (1904): 145–52.

Hall, Samuel. *Lectures on School-Keeping.* Boston: Richardson, Lord, and Holbrook, 1829.

Harris, Barbara. *Beyond Her Sphere: Women and the Professions in American History.* Westport, CT: Greenwood, 1978.

Harris, Joseph. *A Teaching Subject: Composition since 1966.* Englewood Cliffs, NJ: Prentice, 1996.

Haskel, Thomas L., ed. *The Authority of Experts: Studies in History and Theory.* Bloomington: Indiana UP, 1984.

Heath, Shirley Brice. *Ways with Words.* New York: Cambridge UP, 1986.

Henderson, A., and J. Whittier-Ferguson. *U-M Department of English: Graduate Program: Fall 2001 Descriptions: 695.001 Pedagogy.* 24 June 2002. <http://www.lsa.umich.edu/english/grad/descriptions/archive/fall0 1desc.html>.

Hinsdale, B. A. *Horace Mann and the Common School Revival in the United States.* New York: Scribner's, 1937.

Hofstadter, Richard, and Wilson Smith, eds. *American Higher Education: A Documentary History.* Chicago: U of Chicago P, 1961.

Holbrook, Sue Ellen. "Women's Work: The Feminizing of Composition." *Rhetoric Review* 9.2 (1991): 201–29.

Holmes, Madelyn, and Beverly J. Weiss, eds. *Lives of Women Public Schoolteachers: Scenes from American Educational History.* New York: Garland, 1995.

Holmes Partnership. *The Holmes Partnership.* 10 July 2002. <http://www.holmespartnership.org>.

Horner, Bruce. *Terms of Work for Composition: A Materialist Critique.* Albany: State U of New York P, 2000.

———. "Traditions and Professionalization: Reconceiving Work in Composition." *CCC* 51.3 (2000): 366–98.

Hosic, James Fleming. *English Journal* 7.2 (Feb. 1918): 144–45.

Hutcheson, Philo A. *A Professional Professoriate: Unionization, Bureaucratization, and the AAUP.* Nashville: Vanderbilt UP, 2000.

Johnson, Walter R. "Observations on the Improvement of Seminaries of Learning in the United States: With Suggestions for Its Accomplishment." 1825. *American Journal of Education* 5 (1858): 799–802.

Kaestle, Carl F. "The History of Literacy and the History of Readers." *Review of Research in Education* 12 (1985): 11–53.

Kenny, Shirley Strum. Telephone interview. 11 Aug. 2000.

Kimball, Roger. *The "True Professional Ideal" in America: A History.* Cambridge, MA: Blackwell, 1992.

Kirkland, J. H. "The Teacher and the State." *The Annals of the American Academy of Political and Social Science* 22 (July–Dec. 1903): 249–56.

Kliebard, Herbert M. "Education at the Turn of the Century: A Crucible for Curriculum Change." *Educational Researcher* 11 (Jan. 1982): 16–24.

Larson, Magali Sarfatti. *The Rise of Professionalism: A Sociological Analysis.* Berkeley: U of California P, 1977.

Lathrop, Delia A. "The Professional Training of Teachers." *Journal of Proceedings and Addresses of the National Educational Association 1875* (1875): 138–47.

Legatt, T. "Teaching as a Profession." *Professions and Professionalization.* Ed. J. A. Jackson. Cambridge: Cambridge UP, 1970. 153–78.

Lewis, Lionel S. *Marginal Worth: Teaching and the Academic Labor Market.* New Brunswick, NJ: Transaction, 1996.

Lieberman, Myron. *Education as a Profession.* Englewood Cliffs, NJ: Prentice, 1956.

Maid, Barry. "Non-Tenure-Track Instructors at UAR: Breaking Rules, Splitting Departments." Schell and Stock 76–90.

Marshall, Margaret J. "Sites for (Invisible) Intellectual Work." *The Politics of Writing Centers.* Ed. Jane Nelson and Kathy Evertz. Portsmouth, NH: Boynton, 2001. 74–84.

Mattingly, Paul. *The Classless Profession: American Schoolmen in the Nineteenth Century.* New York: New York UP, 1975.

McCormick, Alexander C. *Carnegie Classification 2000: Background and Plans.* Carnegie Classification of Institutions of Higher Education, Carnegie Foundation. 10 Nov. 2000. <http://www.carnegiefoundation.org/Classification/cc2000.html>.

McIver, Alex[ander]. Letter to Kemp P. Battle, President of the University, 24 July 1879. University archives, University of North Carolina, Chapel Hill.

Miller, Richard E. *As If Learning Mattered: Reforming Higher Education.* Ithaca: Cornell UP, 1998.

———. "A Writing Program's Assets Reconsidered: Getting Beyond Impassioned Teachers and Enslaved Workers." *Pedagogy: Critical Approaches to Teaching Literature, Language, Composition, and Culture* 1.2 (Spring 2001): 241–49.

Miller, Susan. "The Feminization of Composition." *The Politics of Writing Instruction: Postsecondary.* Ed. Richard Bullock and John Trimbur. Portsmouth, NH: Boynton, 1991. 39–54.

———. *Textual Carnivals: The Politics of Composition.* Carbondale: Southern Illinois UP, 1991.

MLA Commission on Professional Service. "Making Faculty Work Visible; Reinterpreting Professional Service, Teaching, and Research in the Fields of Language and Literature." *Profession 1996* (1996): 161–216.

MLA Committee on the Status of Women in the Profession. "Women in the Profession." *Profession 2000* (2000): 191–217.

Murphy, Marjorie. *Blackboard Unions: The AFT and the NEA, 1900–1980.* Ithaca: Cornell UP, 1990.

National Center for Education Statistics (NCES). "Table 257. Bachelor's, Master's and Doctoral Degrees Conferred by Degree-Granting Institutions, by Sex of Student and Field of Study: 1997–98." *Digest of Education Statistics 2000.* 28 June 2002. <http://nces.ed.gov/pubs2001/digest/dt257.html>.

———. "Table 287. Earned Degrees in English Language and Literature/Letters Conferred by Degree-Granting Institutions, by Level of Degree and Sex of Student: 1949–50 to 1997–98." *Digest of Education Statistics 2000.* 28 June 2002. <http://nces.ed.gov/pubs2001/digest/dt287.html>.

National Educational Association. *Journal of Proceedings and Addresses of the National Education Association of the United States* (1894).

———. *Proceedings of the International Congress of Education of the World's Columbian Exposition* (1893).

National Science Foundation's Division of Undergraduate Education. *PLTL Workshop Project.* 10 July 2002. <www.sci.ccny.cuny.edu/~chemwksp/index.html>.

Nelson, Cary, ed. *Will Teach for Food: Academic Labor in Crisis.* Minneapolis: U of Minnesota, 1997.

Ohmann, Richard. *Politics of Letters.* Middletown, CT: Wesleyan UP, 1987.

Peirce, Cyrus. "The First Term of Cyrus Peirce, First Principal of the Lexington, Massachusetts, Normal School." *Education in the United States: A Documentary History.* Vol. 3. Ed. Sol Cohen. New York: Random, 1839. 1328–31.

Pytlik, Betty P. "How Graduate Students Were Prepared to Teach Writing—1850–1970." *Preparing College Teachers of Writing: Histories, Theories, Programs, Practices.* Ed. Betty P. Pytlik and Sarah Liggett. New York: Oxford UP, 2002. 3–16.

Resnick, Daniel P., and Lauren B. Resnick. "The Nature of Literacy: An Historical Exploration." *Harvard Educational Review* 47 (1977): 370–85.

Rice, Joseph Mayer. "The Public Schools of Chicago and St. Paul." *Forum* (1893): 200–15.

Samander, Tara. "Re: Annual Business Meeting Motions." E-mail to author. 19 Sept. 2001.

Schell, Eileen. *Gypsy Academic and Mother-Teachers: Gender, Contingent Labor, and Writing Instruction.* Portsmouth, NH: Boynton, 1998.

Schell, Eileen, and Patricia Stock, eds. *Moving a Mountain: Contingent Faculty in Composition.* Urbana, IL: NCTE, 2001.

Scott, Fred Newton. "Editorial: Training and Mistraining." *English Journal* 2.7 (Sept. 1913): 456–58.

Sewall, May Wright. "Woman's Work in Education." *The Journal of Proceedings and Addresses of the National Educational Association 1884* (1884): 153–56.

Shor, Ira. *Culture Wars: School and Society in the Conservative Restoration, 1969–84.* Boston: Routledge and Kegan Paul, 1986.

Sledd, Andrew. "Readin' and Riotin': The Politics of Literacy." *College English* 50.5 (1988): 496–508.

Southern Regional Education Board, Undergraduate Education Reform Project. *Faculty Development Centers in Southern Universities.* Ed. Mary Lynn Crow and Ohmer Milton. Southern Regional Education Board, 1976.

Spellmeyer, Kurt. *Course Descriptions:352:501, Index #02277.* 24 June 2002. <http://english.rutgers.edu/coursesGRAD/2002_FALL_U2002_DES.htm>.

Stedman, Lawrence, and Carl Kaestle. "Literacy and Reading Performance in the United States, from 1880 to the Present." *Reading Research Quarterly* 22.1 (1987): 8–46.

Stober, Myra H., and David Tyack. "Why Do Women Teach and Men Manage? A Report on Research on Schools." *Signs* 5 (1980): 494–503.

Stock, Patricia, Amanda Brown, David Franke, and John Starkweather. "The Scholarship of Teaching: Contributions from Contingent Faculty." Schell and Stock 287–323.

Teacher Quality Enhancement Forum. *Teacher Quality Enhancement Projects.* 12 July 2002. <www.coe.ilstu.edu/iplp/tqeforum.html>.

Trimbur, John. "Literacy and the Discourses of Crisis." *Politics of Writing Instruction: Postsecondary.* Ed. Richard Bullock and John Trimbur. Portsmouth, NH: Boynton, 1991. 277–96.

University of Michigan Department of English, Graduate Program. *Pedagogical Training.* 30 June 2001. <http://www.lsa.umich.edu/english/grad/pedagogical.html>.

University Normal School Announcement for 1881. Chapel Hill: U of North Carolina, 1881.

U.S. Census Bureau. "No. 1425. Education Summary—Enrollment, Graduates, and Degrees: 1900 to 1998, and Projects 1999 and 2000." *Statistical Abstract of the United States: 1999.* 28 June 2002. <http://www.census.gov/prod/99pubs/99statab/sec31.pdf>.

Vance, Zebulon Baird. North Carolina Legislative Documents. 1876–77. File 25. Governor's Message. Chapel Hill: U of North Carolina.

Veysey, L. R. "Higher Education as a Profession: Changes and Continuities." *The*

Professions in American History. Ed. Nathan O. Hatch. Notre Dame, IN: U of Notre Dame P, 1988. 15–32.

Vollmer, H. W., and D. J. Mills, eds. *Professionalization*. Englewood Cliffs, NJ: Prentice, 1966.

Watkins, Evan. *Work Time: English Departments and the Circulation of Cultural Value*. Stanford, CA: Stanford UP, 1989.

Weiss, Beverly J. "Student and Teacher at the First State Normal School in the US: Electa Lincoln Walton, 1824–1908." *Lives of Women Public Schoolteachers: Scenes from American Educational History*. Ed. Madelyn Holmes and Beverly J. Weiss. New York: Garland, 1995. 31–52.

White, Hayden. *The Content of the Form: Narrative Discourse and Historical Representation*. Baltimore: Johns Hopkins UP, 1987.

White, James Boyd. *Justice as Translation: An Essay in Cultural and Legal Criticism*. Chicago: U of Chicago P, 1990.

Wilson, Louis R. "Allying the University with the Public Schools." *The University of North Carolina, 1900–1930: The Making of a Modern University*. Chapel Hill: U of North Carolina P, 1957. 84–92.

Wright, Arthur D., and George E. Gardner, eds. *Hall's Lectures on School-Keeping with Notes*. Hanover, NH: Dartmouth UP, 1929.

Index

AAUP (American Association of University Professors), distinction between labor unions and, 109–11
AFL (American Federation of Labor): teachers and, 113; Yale graduate teaching assistants and, 120
African Americans as teachers, 53, 55
AFT (American Federation of Teachers), 111, 112
Alcott, Mr. (of Germantown), 47
Allen, Harold, 81–82
American Association of University Professors. *See* AAUP
American Federation of Labor. *See* AFL
American Institute of Instruction, 40, 46–49; women in, 46–48
American universities: attendance at, 9, 13, 68, 122; as common schooling, 9, 16, 43, 63–64, 70–71, 79–80, 145, 165; creation of, 7–8, 12, 14–15. *See also* higher education
Apple, Michael, 46, 49
Arizona State University, 125
As If Learning Mattered: Reforming Higher Education (Miller), 147–48

Badger, Reid, 51
Barnard, Henry, 20, 55
Becker, Howard S., 11
Beecher, Catherine, 44–46, 77
Bérubé, Michael, 121–22, 148
Bicknell, Thomas W., 1
Bledstein, Burton, 11, 13
Boston Patriot, 28
Boyer, Ernest, 64–65, 132–34
Boyer report, 18, 137, 170; composition and, 66–67, 72, 76; focus of, on research universities, 90–92; and formation of commission, 18, 64–65; foundation sponsorship of, 64–66; similarity of, to earlier documents, 67–68, 70–72; and training of graduate students as teachers, 71–76, 89–90
Brackett, Anna C., 47
Brereton, John, 8, 124, 148, 150
Brown, Amanda, 138
Brumberger, Eva, 137
bureaucracy: features of, 108–9, 164; material conditions and, 121, 127–28, 147–48; schools as, 3, 30, 94; teaching and, 139, 143
Butler, Nicholas, 113, 116
Butler, Vera, 28, 40, 43
Button, H. Warren, 43

Calhoun, W. B., 29
Carnegie Foundation, 132; Boyer Commission and, 64–66; classification of higher education by, 69–70
Carr-Saunders, A. M., 10
Carter, James, 26, 28, 31–35, 38–39, 68
Carter, Susan, 52
CCCC (Conference on College Composition and Communication): Commission on the Status of Women, 107; graduate students and, 81–82; 1952 Committee on Composition Teaching, 124; non-tenure-track debate in, 105–8; Professional Equity Project of, 105–8; women in, 107–8, 131
character: professionals and, 12, 32, 57; of schools, 32, 74; of teachers, 22, 26, 31–32, 37–38, 57, 74
Chicago Teachers Federation. *See* CTF
Child, Francis James, 8, 14
class: anxiety and literacy crisis, 6, 9,

18; bias, 3, 155; differences in, 152; literacy practices and, 5–6, 24, 151; of professionals, 12, 73, 122; of teachers, 19, 22–27, 42–43, 49, 58, 62, 69, 116, 144, 166; of university faculty, 11–12, 73, 122–23; uses of schooling by, 9, 52–54, 151–52; values 11, 19, 53–54

clergy, 23–24; as professional ideal, 12–13

Clifford, Geraldine Joncich, 5–7

Clinton, President Bill, 9, 151, 155

Cohen, Sol, 38, 42

collaboration: interdisciplinary, 156–57; as professional value, 136; in scholarship, 177–78; between teachers, 162–65

colleges: admission to, 22; early American, 7–8; gender in, 51–53. *See also* higher education

common schooling: higher education as, 9, 16, 43, 63–64, 70–71, 79–80, 145, 165; literacy and, 3–4, 6; teachers and, 13, 20–27, 28–44, 56–61

composition: as apprenticeship, 124–25; Boyer report and, 66–67, 72, 76; disciplinary status of, 16, 131–32, 147, 149, 166; faculty in, 64, 76, 93, 95–108, 124–32, 137–42, 144, 146–49, 154–56, 161–65; feminization of, 15, 127–31, 146, 151; at Harvard, 8, 12, 14–15; interdisciplinary connections of, 156–57, 160–61; literacy and, 2–4, 7–9, 12, 16, 86–87, 142, 148, 150–52, 154, 156–57, 160–67, 171; literature and, 8, 12, 14, 16, 72, 76, 86, 99–103, 129, 148, 171; prejudices against, 2, 8, 124–25, 131–32, 143, 147–48, 150, 165, 171; preparation for teaching, 76–90, 123–27, 153, 163, 167, 169, 171–73; requirement for, 12, 56, 146, 152, 156; scholarship in, 157, 177–79; as teaching subject, 125–28; women in, 103, 128–31

Conference on College Composition and Communication. *See* CCCC

contingent faculty. *See* non-tenure-track faculty

Cox, John Harrington, 72

Cremin, Lawrence, 7

CTF (Chicago Teachers Federation), 112–16, 119; and AFL, 113

doctorates, statistics about, 52, 72, 129–30

doctor of arts degree, 80

Duke University, 157, 161

Ehrenreich, Barbara, 15, 29

Ehrenreich, John, 15, 29

Eliot, Charles W., 8, 12, 14

Ellery, Josephine, 48

Elsbree, Willard S., 40, 55, 60

Enos, Theresa, 128

Essays upon Popular Education with an Outline of an Institution for the Education of Teachers (Carter), 28

Fawcett, Millicent Garrett, 50

Fish, Stanley, 15, 122

Franke, David, 138

Freidson, Eliot, 10

Friend of Liberty, 20–26, 31

Fries, Charles C., 81

Gaff, Jerry G., 170

Gallagher, Chris, 87–88, 168

Geiger, Roger, 8–9

gender. *See* teachers, male versus female; women

Gere, Anne Ruggles, 176

Glenn, Cheryl, 151, 155–56

graduate students: assistantships for, 125–26; Boyer report and, 67, 71–76, 89–91; CCCC and, 81–82; connections of, to labor union at Yale, 120–22, 123–24; MLA and, 78; NCTE and, 78; non-tenure-track positions and, 104–5; preparation of, as teachers, 64, 67, 71–92, 123,

126–28, 131, 170–75; as skilled labor, 169; as teachers, 82, 104–5; as university faculty, 71–76, 104–5, 120–25, 147, 160–61
Green, Steven, 99, 104
Greenough, Chester Noyes, 77–78
Griggs, Irwin, 124
Guinier, Lani, 151, 155
Gypsy Academic and Mother-Teachers (Schell), 146

Haber, Samuel, 10
Haley, Margaret, 93–94, 112–16, 119, 138, 147
Hall, Samuel Reed, 37–40, 68
Harper bill, 116, 119
Harris, Barbara, 13, 51–52
Harris, Joseph, 127
Harris, William T., 47, 50
Harvard University: composition at, 8, 12, 14–15; graduate students as teachers at, 82
Haskel, Thomas L., 10
Hayward, Mrs. (of South Boston), 47
Heath, Shirley Brice, 151
Henderson, A., 84–85
higher education: attendance in, 122; classification of, 69–70, 90; commodification of, 141; as common schooling, 9, 16, 43, 63–64, 70–71, 79–80, 145, 165; degrees awarded in, 67, 90, 129; early American colleges and, 7–8; faculty in, 68, 108–11, 170–71; labor unions in, 108–11, 120–22, 146; literacy in, 3, 7–9, 91; material conditions in, 94–108, 123, 138, 145–50; non-tenure-track faculty in, 93, 130, 149–50; public criticism of, 3, 16, 63–68, 74, 145, 148, 176; as qualification for teaching, 24. *See also* American universities; colleges; normal schools; *and names of specific institutions*
Hill, Adams Sherman, 8, 15
Hill, Anita, 151, 155
Hinsdale, B. A., 26

Hofstadter, Richard, 7
Holbrook, Sue Ellen, 128
Holmes, Madelyn, 42, 53–54
Holmes Partnerships, 174
Horner, Bruce, 141, 165–66
Hosic, James Fleming, 80–81
Hughes, Miss E. P., 49
Hutcheson, Philo A. 108–11
Hyde, Ellen, 53–54

Indiana University of Pennsylvania, 125
intellectual work, 141, 158–59
interdisciplinarity, 172; in composition, 156–57, 160–61
International Congress of Education, 49
International Educational Series, 47

James, William, 113
Johnson, Walter, 33–39, 68
Jones, Frank L., 40
Journal of Education, 38

Kaestle, Carl F., 4, 6
Kenny, Shirley Strum, 64–66
Kimball, Roger, 12–13, 15, 23, 25, 40
Kirkland, Dr. J. H., 41
Kliebard, Herbert M., 7

labor: AAUP and, 109–11; Chicago teachers and, 111–20; graduate students as, 120–24, 169; higher education and, 94, 108–11, 120–22; NEA resolution on, 116–18; opposition to "profession," 108, 111, 113, 119, 121, 139, 142, 144, 155, 169–70, 179; professional organizations and, 108–11, 113–14, 147; rhetoric of, 3, 113, 119, 137–38, 142, 144, 147, 150; teaching and, 113, 122, 131–32, 137, 139, 144, 147, 161–62, 165–66
Larson, Magali Sarfatti, 10
Lathrop, Delia A., 1–2
law, as professional ideal, 13
Lectures on School-Keeping (Hall), 37–39

Legatt, T., 12
Lewis, Lionel S., 131–32
Lieberman, Myron, 48
literacy: composition and, 2–4, 7–9, 12, 16, 86–87, 142, 148, 150–52, 154, 156–57, 160–67, 171; consciousness, 6, 18–19; crisis, 6–7; definitions of 4–5, 7, 9, 149; economic prosperity and, 18; evolution of, 4–9; in higher education, 3, 7–9, 63, 142; level of, 32, 63; middle class anxiety and, 6; public criticism and, 10, 63, 176–78; rates of, 6–7; schooling and, 4–9; in teacher preparation programs, 19, 22–23, 41–43, 53–54, 57–60, 74, 77
literature, 156; composition and, 8, 12, 14, 16, 72, 76, 86, 99–103, 129, 148, 171; in teacher preparation programs, 37, 53, 79, 124

Maid, Barry, 138
Mann, Horace, 26
Marginal Worth: Teaching and the Academic Labor Market (Lewis), 131–32
Marshall, Margaret, 134
Massachusetts Magazine, 20
material conditions: construction of, as not professional concern, 16, 36, 114, 121–22, 137–42, 144, 166; of higher education 108, 123, 137–42, 145–50, 164; improving, 94, 132, 142; maternity leave and, 93–108; of non-tenure-track hiring, 99–103; schools and, 30; of teaching, 3, 44, 75, 91–92, 93–94, 111–13, 123, 138–39
Mattingly, Paul, 13
McIver, Alexander, 57–58
Miller, Richard, 131–32, 147–50
Miller, Susan, 8, 12, 15, 128–29
MLA (Modern Language Association), 86, 166; Commission on Professional Service, 135–37, 158, 166; Committee on the Preparation of College Teachers, 78; Committee on the Status of Women in the Profession, 129–30; survey on preparing graduate students as teachers, 78; Yale grade strike and, 120–22
Moving a Mountain: Transforming the Role of Contingent Faculty in Composition Studies and Higher Education (Schell and Stock), 93, 137–39
Murphy, Marjorie, 112, 115–16, 119

National Council of Teachers of English. *See* NCTE
National Educational Association. *See* NEA
National Science Foundation's Division of Undergraduate Education, 174
Native Americans, in normal schools, 53
NCTE (National Council of Teachers of English): Committee on the Preparation of College Teachers, 78–81; report on teaching seminars, 76–77
NEA (National Education Association): 1884 meeting of, 1; 1894 resolution of, on labor conflicts, 116–18; 1910 survey of teachers by, 40–41; classroom teachers and, 118–19; Haley's speech to, 93–94, 113–14; required membership in, 115; teachers' unions and, 113–15
Nelson, Cary, 123–24, 131, 148, 150
non-tenure-track faculty: AAUP and, 110–11; CCCC debate about, 105–8; duties of, 100; evaluation of, for promotion, 138, 164; full-time versus part-time, 99–103; graduate students as, 104–5; hiring of, 99–103, 155; material conditions and, 93–108, 137–42, 146–50; maternity leave for, 95–99; number of women among, 103, 129–31; as professionals, 167, 169
normal schools: curriculum of, 41–42, 53–54, 56–58; principals of, 13–14, 41–43, 53–54; state-supported, 40, 53, 55, 58; statistics about, 40–

41, 43–44; students in, 41–44, 53. *See also* teacher seminaries; teachers' institutes

Ohmann, Richard, 7

Parker, Colonel Francis, 113
Patterson, Annabel, 120–22
Peabody, Elizabeth, 47
Peabody funds, 58
pedagogical training. *See* teachers, education of; teaching, seminars
peer-led teaching initiative, 174–75
Peirce, Cyrus, 14, 41–43, 57
Perkins, Miss (of Bath, Maine), 48
Pew Foundation, 65, 170
professionalization: class and, 37–39, 52–53, 61–62, 63–64, 67–68; criticism of, 15, 122–23; of graduate students, 71–90, 123–24, 123–35, 171–76; as response to public criticism, 3, 16–17, 18–20, 29–31, 176; studies of, 10, 108–11
professional organizations, 40, 42, 46, 49, 52, 54, 55, 78, 94, 158; labor unions and, 108–11, 114–15, 147; women in, 1–2, 46–51. *See also names of specific organizations*
professionals: bureaucracy and, 3, 94, 108–11, 143–44, 147–51; character of, 12, 32, 57; development of, 162–65, 167, 170; features of, 10–13, 25–27, 36, 48, 108–11, 131–32, 158–60, 164; ideal, 12–13, 23–25; rhetoric of, 3, 18, 34, 68–69, 114–20, 121–23, 137–42, 165–66; values of, 11, 25, 34, 94, 121, 136, 158–59, 176–79; women and, 13–14, 48
Professions, The (Carr-Saunders and Wilson), 10
professors, as professional ideal, 13
Provenzo, Eugene F., Jr., 43
Prus, Mark, 52
public criticism: of education, 6–7, 18–20, 61, 115; of higher education, 3, 16, 63, 63–68, 74, 145, 148, 176; literacy and, 10, 63, 176–78; of teachers, 3, 9–10, 19, 28, 30, 55–56
Purdue University, 125
Pytlik, Betty P., 64

"Reinventing Undergraduate Education: A Blueprint for America's Research Universities." *See* Boyer report
Resnick, Daniel P., 7
Resnick, Lauren B., 7
rhetoric: Boylston Chair of, 14; composition and, 8, 21, 23, 91, 101, 125, 126, 129, 131, 148, 156, 160, 169; of crisis, 6, 29, 67–68, 74; inherited, 2–3, 18, 68–71, 122–23, 136–37, 143–46; of labor, 3, 16, 113–22, 137–38, 142; of professionalism, 18, 46, 57, 63, 71–75, 113, 119, 127, 165–66; of professionals, 150, 177; of reform, 16–19, 66; of silence, 47–48, 151, 155
Rhetoric Review, survey of doctoral programs in, 125–26, 130–31
Rice, Joseph Mayer, 115
Robbins, Miss (of Hartford, Connecticut), 47
Rutgers University, teaching seminars, 85–87

Schell, Eileen, 128, 93, 128, 137, 146–47, 149–50
scholarship: collaboration in, 177–78; composition and, 157–59, 175–79; teaching and, 3, 16, 36, 57–58, 65–66, 92–94, 97–99, 108, 124–38, 141, 144, 148, 158, 161–62, 166, 170–71
schooling: as bureaucracy, 30, common, 3, 9, 13, 16, 19, 21–23, 41, 43, 63–64, 70–71, 79–80, 145–46, 165; definition of, 20; individual merit and, 6; literacy and, 4–9; numbers in attendance at, 7, 9; opportunities for, 6; political corruption in, 115;

Index

scholarship of, 66, uses of, by class, 9, 52–54, 151–52
school keeping. *See* teaching
School Magazine, The, 38
Scott, Fred Newton, 77
Selfe, Cynthia, 105
Sewall, May Wright, 1–2
Shor, Ira, 7, 105–6
Shulman, Lee, 132
Simpson, Ronald D., 170
Sledd, Andrew, 7
Smith, Wilson, 7
Spellmeyer, Kurt, 85–87, 169
Starkweather, John, 138
Stedman, Lawrence, 4
Stober, Myra H., 46
Stock, Patricia, 93, 137, 138, 167
SUCCEED Project, 174, 175
Suggestions Respecting Improvements in Education (Beecher), 45–46

Teacher Quality Enhancement, 174–75
teachers: character and, 22, 26, 31–32, 37–38, 57, 74; and class distinctions, 19, 22–27, 36, 42–43, 49, 52, 58, 62, 69, 116, 144, 166; collaboration among, 162–65; criticism of, 3, 9–10, 19–32, 55–56, 67–69; devaluing of, 12–13; education of, 2, 3, 10, 20–25, 29–43, 54–62, 64, 71–92, 123–28, 131, 162–65, 170–76; evaluation of, 36, 139–40; graduate students as, 82, 104–5; labor and, 111–20; male versus female, 13, 43–44; memoirs of, 124; NEA and, 118–19; numbers of, needed, 20, 40–41, 56; professional development of, 153, 163, 167–71; professional status of, 3, 10, 24, 43, 54, 60–62, 64, 77, 80, 114, 145; role of, 53, 112; salaries of, 43; testing of, 57–58; unionization and, 93, 111–23, 146–47; women and, 13, 24, 39, 43–44, 115–16; women's clubs and, 116
teacher seminaries: earliest call for, 20–27; essentials of, 31–32; Samuel Hall's, 37–40; improving, 33–37; state-supported, 40; women in, 39, 40, 44. *See also* normal schools; teachers' institutes
teachers' institutes, 54–62; curricula of, 56–57, 59–60. *See also* normal schools; teacher seminaries; teaching, seminars
teaching: circles, 113; definition of, 19–20, 27, 30–39, 42–44, 52, 55–57, 60–61, 64, 74, 79–80, 85, 87, 88–97, 125, 127–28, 132–37, 139–41, 144; evaluation of, 132, 139–41; feminization of, 13, 44–46, 51, 80, 128, 147, 151; as intellectual work, 135–36, 138, 162–65, 176; material conditions of, 93, 108; as mothering, 46, 140; as a profession, 29; and professional values, 25, 34; the public, 176–79; scholarship and, 3, 92, 94, 123–37, 171; seminars, 20–25, 76–90, 126, 128, 171; status of, 34, 90, 92, 94; as women's work, 14, 19–20, 128–29, 144; as work, 89
Thomas, Clarence, 151
Trimber, John, 6
tutoring, 159
Tyack, David, 46
Tyler, H. W., 109–10

unionization: classroom teachers and, 93–94, 111–23, 146–47; university faculty and, 110–11
university faculty: attitudes of, toward school teachers, 111; attitudes of, toward workers, 122–23; criticism of, 67–69; definitions of, 90, 100, 104–5, 109, 122, 138–39, 163, 169; development programs for, 64; evaluations of, 159; gender of, by rank in composition, 130–31; graduate students as, 71–76, 104–5, 120–25; non-tenure-track positions among, 2, 93–108, 110–11, 123, 129–30, 146, 149, 167; as professionals, 120–21, 139, 148–49; reward sys-

tems, 67, 71, 80, 127, 135–37, 138–41, 149, 157–60, 177–78; senate, 98–100, 104; status of, 109; tenure-track positions among, 129–30; unionization and, 110–11; work of, 16, 72, 82–83, 89, 97–98, 134–37, 147, 158, 162, 169–71, 176–77

University of Illinois, 157; graduate students as teachers in, 82

University of Iowa, 160

University of Michigan, 174; English and Education program, 174; teaching seminars, 81, 82–85, 168

University of Nebraska, teaching seminars, 87–88

University of North Carolina: at Chapel Hill, 55, 56, 58–59; at Fayetteville, 55; teacher education programs in, 56–60

University of Syracuse, 156, 167

Vance, Governor Zebulon Baird, 55–57
Veysey, L. R., 7
Vollmer, H. W., 10

Walton, Electa Lincoln, 14
Watkins, Evan, 141
Ways with Words (Heath), 151

Weiss, Beverly J., 14, 42, 53–54
Wells, Kate Gannett, 54
White, Hayden, 69
White, James Boyd, 150
Whittier-Ferguson, J., 84–85
Wilson, Louis R., 55, 58–59
Wilson, P. A., 10
women: in composition, 15–16, 103, 128–31; and "cult of domesticity," 51; degrees earned by, 129–30; education of, 1–2, 9, 39–40, 44, 53–54; in higher education, 2, 103, 129–31; maternity leave for, 95–99; pay rates for, 43–44, 52; as principals, 13–14, 45–46, 53–54; professional status of, 14, 19, 46–52; role in professional organizations, 1–2, 46–51, 107–8, 119, 129–31; as teachers, 13–14, 19–20, 24, 31, 39, 43–45, 51–52, 115–16, 127, 143–44; teachers' institutes for, 55–58; tenure of, 105–8, 130–31; in the workplace, 51–52
World's Columbian Exposition, 49–51
WPA (Writing Program Administrators), evaluating intellectual work, 158–59

Yale, grade strike at, 120–23
Young, Ella Flagg, 48

MARGARET J. MARSHALL is an associate professor of English at the University of Miami, where she serves as the director of the English Composition Program, teaches the required graduate seminar in teaching composition for new teaching assistants, and offers courses in rhetoric, composition, and women's literature. Her first book, *Contesting Cultural Rhetorics: Public Discourse and Education, 1890–1900*, focuses on the cultural constructions of *education* as a key term in American public discourse. She contributed a chapter to the award-winning collection *The Politics of Writing Centers*. Her articles analyzing the rhetoric of various forms of educational discourses have been published in *College Composition and Communication, English Education,* and the *Iowa Journal of Rhetoric.*

Studies in Writing & Rhetoric

In 1980 the Conference on College Composition and Communication established the Studies in Writing & Rhetoric (SWR) series as a forum for monograph-length arguments or presentations that engage general compositionists. SWR encourages extended essays or research reports addressing any issue in composition and rhetoric from any theoretical or research perspective as long as the general significance to the field is clear. Previous SWR publications serve as models for prospective authors; in addition, contributors may propose alternate formats and agendas that inform or extend the field's current debates.

SWR is particularly interested in projects that connect the specific research site or theoretical framework to contemporary classroom and institutional contexts of direct concern to compositionists across the nation. Such connections may come from several approaches, including cultural, theoretical, field-based, gendered, historical, and interdisciplinary. SWR especially encourages monographs by scholars early in their careers, by established scholars who wish to share an insight or exhortation with the field, and by scholars of color.

The SWR series editor and editorial board members are committed to working closely with prospective authors and offering significant developmental advice for encouraged manuscripts and prospectuses. Editorships rotate every five years. Prospective authors intending to submit a prospectus during the 2002 to 2007 editorial appointment should obtain submission guidelines from Robert Brooke, SWR editor, University of Nebraska–Lincoln, Department of English, P.O. Box 880337, 202 Andrews Hall, Lincoln, NE 68588-0337.

General inquiries may also be addressed to Sponsoring Editor, Studies in Writing & Rhetoric, Southern Illinois University Press, P.O. Box 3697, Carbondale, IL 62902-3697.